Keyboard Skills for Music Educators

Keyboard Skills for Music Educators: Score Reading is the first textbook that provides the depth of material and insight of seasoned music educators to equip future educators with the ability to play from an open score at the keyboard. Score reading can be a daunting prospect for even the most accomplished pianist, but it is a skill required of all choral and instrumental music instructors. Although most music education curricula include requirements to achieve a certain level of proficiency in open score reading, standard textbooks contain very little material devoted to developing this skill.

This textbook provides a gradual and graded approach, progressing from two-part reading to four or more parts in a variety of clefs. Each chapter focuses on one grouping of voices and provides many musical examples from a broad sampling of choral and instrumental repertoire ranging from Renaissance to contemporary works.

Shellie Gregorich is Associate Professor of Music Theory and Piano and serves as Department Chair at Mansfield University of Pennsylvania.

Benjamin Moritz is an active performer and teacher and directs the Honors Program at Metropolitan State College of Denver.

Keyboard Skills for Music Educators

Score Reading

Shellie Gregorich

Mansfield University

and

Benjamin Moritz

Metropolitan State College of Denver

Routledge
Taylor & Francis Group

NEW YORK AND LONDON

Routledge
New York & London

First published 2012
by Routledge
711 Third Avenue, New York, NY 10017

Simultaneously published in the UK
by Routledge
2 Park Square, Milton Park, Abingdon, Oxon OX14 4RN

Routledge is an imprint of the Taylor & Francis Group, an informa business

© 2012 Taylor & Francis

The right of Shellie Gregorich and Benjamin Moritz to be identified as authors of this work has been asserted by them in accordance with sections 77 and 78 of the Copyright, Designs and Patents Act 1988.

Library of Congress Cataloging in Publication Data
A catalog record has been requested for this book
Gregorich, Shellie.
   Keyboard skills for music educators : score reading / Shellie Gregorich and Benjamin Moritz.
      p. cm.
   Includes index.
   1. Score reading and playing. 2. Keyboard instruments--Instruction and study.
   I. Moritz, Benjamin. II. Title.
   MT85.G79 2011
   786'.1423—dc22   2011003616

ISBN13: 978-0-415-88897-4 (hbk)
ISBN13: 978-0-415-88898-1 (pbk)
ISBN13: 978-0-203-80808-5 (ebk)

Typeset in Caslon by
Keystroke, Station Road, Codsall, Wolverhampton

Printed and bound in the United States of America on acid-free paper
by Edward Brothers Inc.

Table of Contents

Preface

The Unique Challenges of Reading Open Score

Sitting down at the keyboard to play from an open score can be a daunting prospect for even the most accomplished pianist. Simply put, reading four or more staves simultaneously requires a different skill set than most pianists ever develop. To make things worse, it is rarely professional pianists that encounter situations in which they are asked to play open scores—it is choral and instrumental conductors for whom piano is only a secondary instrument! For conductors who may play standard, grand staff accompaniments with some trepidation, the request (or demand!) to perform from a full score can cause full-fledged panic. The reason for this panic comes from a lack of adequate training in the unique demands of open score performance.

It is the aim of *Keyboard Skills for Music Educators: Score Reading* to help aspiring conductors acquire these important skills.

Goals

Just as beginning piano students struggle to read from two staves simultaneously, the transition to four or more staves can be equally difficult. *Keyboard Skills for Music Educators: Score Reading* is designed to ease you into the process, and provide you ample opportunity to develop and hone your new-found skills. Throughout the text you will find tips for processing the large amount of information included in open scores, suggestions for effectively reducing scores when necessary, and explanations of possible contexts in which various scorings might be found.

Being able to sit at a keyboard and play from an open score is a highly important skill for any conductor to possess, and being able to accomplish that task with confidence brings numerous rewards:

- Performing parts for your ensemble helps speed up their preparation process
- Reducing the amount of time needed to prepare open score performances gives you more time to prepare your rehearsals
- Your confidence at the keyboard can give you more confidence throughout your conducting
- Demonstrating your fluency at the podium and the keyboard creates more confidence within your student group as well.

Challenges to Reading Open Scores

What follows is a brief accounting of the unique challenges open score reading presents, and some techniques to equip you in your learning.

Sufficient exposure

Although most music education curricula include requirements to achieve a certain level of proficiency in open score reading at the keyboard, standard keyboard skills texts contain very little material devoted to developing this skill. At most, general texts will include a few examples towards the end of the book, or possibly an appendix with one or two examples for each common grouping.

The philosophy behind this text is that reading open scores requires different skills than reading from a grand staff, and these skills must be addressed in some detail, allowing students to have many opportunities to practice this new format. Therefore, instead of a few open score excerpts at the back of the book, *Keyboard Skills for Music Educators: Score Reading* includes a wide array of exercises that progress from simple two part reading to full instrumental scores.

Clear Learning Outcomes

Although most music educators agree that conductors must possess the ability to perform open scores at the keyboard, detailed standards are few and far between, and vary widely from institution to institution.

This text is organized by specific groupings of voicings, and faculty and institutions can easily choose which areas to cover within their courses.

Sight-Reading

Although sight-reading is an important aspect of keyboard stills, existing texts do not address it. In real-world situations, conductors can usually allow themselves time to prepare for playing an open score before a rehearsal, but unforeseen ensemble problems invariably arise that require them to perform an excerpt at sight. A text that treats open scores as an exclusively pre-prepared skill fails to equip conductors for real-world contexts.

For each chapter, excerpts are included for week-long preparation, and shorter, simpler excerpts are included for sight-reading practice. Additionally, specific techniques are discussed to help quickly process open scores and prepare conductors to create effective performances at sight.

How to Use This Book

Instructors

- **Where to Begin?** Each chapter is intended to be self-contained, thereby allowing instructors to begin with the chapter most appropriate to their students. For example, if students in your course are already familiar with two-part scores containing tenor parts, you could begin the course with Chapter 3, go on to Chapter 4, skip Chapter 5, and then continue with the book.

- **Fingerings:** These are provided sparingly, generally in the beginnings of chapters where new challenges have been introduced. The authors believe that students can benefit from developing their own fingerings, but some instructors may prefer to indicate fingerings in more detail than the text provides.
- **Course Pacing:** For juniors and seniors who have already had two years of class piano, instructors may want to introduce a new chapter each week. For students with less piano background, the materials in this book might be spread out over an entire academic year. Enough sight-reading examples have been provided to allow for both in-class sight-reading, and exercises to be studied independently as well. Although music educators will occasionally be asked to sight-read open scores, at other times they will have days if not weeks to prepare, and therefore we have also included longer exercises at the end of each chapter.
- **In the Classroom:** Because steady tempos and clear metric pulses are so important for ensemble directors, we sought to reinforce this concept throughout the text. To further support this idea, instructors are encouraged to tap or count out loud as the class plays through these exercises. Many students find it hard to go on after playing a wrong note, but for the purposes of leading a musical group, it is frequently true that "The wrong note at the right time is better than the right note at the wrong time!"
- **Page Turns:** Although page turns within excerpts have been minimized, the authors have included some examples that require page turns to gradually expose students to this reality of score reading. Some instructors may choose to allow for a short pause while the page is turned, but students should understand that real-world situations call for pianists to execute page-turns without sacrificing the tempo or dropping a beat.

Students

As you begin your open score studies, take full advantage of the numerous exercises provided in this text. The only way to improve at score reading is . . . to do a lot of score reading! For the sight-reading examples, be sure to select a tempo that allows for a high level of accuracy, while simultaneously challenging you to stay focused. Once you have chosen a tempo, STICK TO IT! If you find it difficult to maintain a tempo, and frequently find that your ending tempo is significantly faster or slower than you began the exercise, use a metronome. For the prepared exercises, do not be afraid to work on small sections until you can play them fluently. Running from the beginning to the end over and over is ineffective at correcting mistakes or unintended pauses. Remember, the primary reason you are learning to read from an open score is so you can lead your musical group. A steady tempo is of vital importance, and should be one of your main goals with any assignment in this text.

Acknowledgments

We would like to thank the reviewers who provided wonderful feedback on the text throughout its development. Their input was extremely important to creating this text and selecting the most useful and appropriate musical excerpts. We would also like to thank the wonderful editorial staff at Taylor & Francis, including Constance Ditzel, Denny Tek, and Jacqueline Dias. Their expertise and professionalism was invaluable in translating our pedagogical ideas from the blackboard to the printed page. Finally, we would like to thank the music students at Mansfield University, many of whom were our guinea pigs as we tested various incarnations of this text in our piano classes. Their feedback and evaluations were helpful in discovering the most effective way to address the challenges of open score reading.

We are grateful to the following authors, composers, publishers, and agents who have granted permission for use of their copyrighted material, listed below in order of appearance.

Chapter 1

Page 7, Ex. 1.6. "Jimmie's Got a Goil." By Vincent Persichetti and E.E. Cummings. Copyright © 1949 (renewed) by G. Schirmer, Inc. (ASCAP). International Copyright Secured. All Rights Reserved.

Chapter 2

Page 33, Ex. 2.19. Spiritual, "This Train," Arranged by Kirby Shaw. Courtesy of Kirby Shaw. www.kirbyshaw.com.
Page 34, Ex. 2.20. "The Clouds." By Cynthia Grey. © 1983 Heritage Music Press, a division of the Lorenz Corporation. All Rights Reserved.

Chapter 3

Page 49, Ex. 3.16. "Liza Jane," Traditional. Arranged by Everett Covin. Copyright © MCMLXXXIII by Alfred Music Publishing Co., Inc. All Rights Reserved. Used by Permission of Alfred Music Publishing Co., Inc.

Chapter 4

Page 57, Ex. 4.7. Arranged by Hayes, "Go Down Moses," mm. 45–52. © Hinshaw Music, Inc. Used with permission.

Page 69, Ex. 4.19. "A Girl's Garden." By Randall Thompson. © 1960, 1988 by E.C. Schirmer Music Company, a division of ECS Publishing, Boston, MA. Used by permission.

Chapter 5

Page 78, Ex. 5.6. "Say Ye to the Righteous," from *The Peacable Kingdom*. By Randall Thompson. © by E.C. Schirmer Music Company, a division of ECS Publishing, Boston, MA. Used by permission.

Page 91, Ex. 5.23. *Maggie and Milly and Molly and May* by Vincent Persichetti. Copyright © 1966 by Elkan-Vogel, Inc. International copyright secured. All rights reserved. Used with permission by Theodore Presser Company.

Chapter 6

Page 102, Ex. 6.12. "Shake the Papaya Down" (21-20222). Arranged by Judith M. Waller and Ruth E. Dwyer. Copyright © 1994 Plymouth Music Co., Inc. Copyright © 2000. Transferred Colla Voce Music, Inc.

Chapter 8

Page 134, Ex. 8.3. Leavett, "Old Man Tucker," mm. 7–12. Old Dan Tucker. Traditional. Arranged by John Leavitt. Copyright © 2000 by HAL LEONARD CORPORATION. International Copyright Secured. All Rights Reserved. Reprinted by permission of Hal Leonard Corporation.

Page 139, Ex. 8.9. "Joshua Fit the Battle of Jericho," Traditional. Arranged by Kirby Shaw. Courtesy of Kirby Shaw. www.kirbyshaw.com.

Page 142, Ex. 8.13. "The Pasture." By Randall Thompson. ©1960, 1988 by E.C. Schirmer Music Company, a division of ECS Publishing, Boston, MA. Used by permission.

Page 147, Ex. 8.18. "The Corinthians." By Ned Rorem. Copyright © 1960, renewed 1988, by Henmar Press, Inc. Used by permission C.F. Peters Corporation. All Rights Reserved.

Chapter 9

Page 168, Ex. 9.13. "The Birds' Noel." By Katherine K. Davis. © 1965, 1993 by Galaxy Music Corporation, a division of ECS Publishing, Boston, MA. Used by permission.

Chapter 11

Page 209, Ex. 11.15. "Hick's Farewell" from *Five American Folk Songs*. Arranged by Samuel Adler. © 1961 (Renewed) WB Music Corp. All Rights Reserved. Used by Permission of Alfred Music Publishing Co., Inc.
Page 212, Ex. 11.17. "Prayers of Kierkegaard", Op. 30. By Samuel Barber. Copyright © 1954 (Renewed) by G. Schirmer, Inc. (ASCAP). International Copyright Secured. All Rights Reserved. Used by permission.

Chapter 12

Page 215, Ex. 12.1. "The Birds' Noel." By Katherine K. Davis. © 1965, 1993 by Galaxy Music Corporation, a division of ECS Publishing, Boston, MA. Used by permission.
Page 236, Ex. 12.14. "The Corinthians." By Ned Rorem. Copyright © 1960, renewed 1988, by Henmar Press, Inc. Used by permission C.F. Peters Corporation. All Rights Reserved.

Chapter 15

Page 285, Ex. 15.10. "Divertimento No. 18" for flute and saxophone." By Paul Arma. © 1989 Gérard Billaudot Editeur SA, Paris France.
Page 290, Ex. 15.13. "Sarabande" from *Eclectic Trio*. By Catherine McMichael. Courtesy of ALRY Publications, Etc., Inc.

Chapter 16

Page 304, Ex. 16.16. Ewazen, Colchester Fantasy, movt. II, "The Marquis of Granby," mm. 1–23. © Southern Music Company. Used with permission.

Part 1

Two and Three Part Reading in Traditional Clefs

<h1>Chapter 1</h1>

<h1>Two Parts: Treble/Bass</h1>

1 Introduction

Two-part open scores that use one treble clef and one bass clef are very similar to traditional piano music on the grand staff. Because most music educators have some experience reading piano music, this open score format is an excellent place to begin. You will encounter this format in choral music scored generally for women (treble clef) and men (bass clef), or more specific scorings such as soprano-bass, or alto-bass. Other instances might include two-part excerpts from larger scores, or instrumental duets.

Visually, the differences between a treble/bass open score and a piano grand staff are slight.

- The grand staff includes an arched bracket grouping the treble and bass staves into one system, while a typical open score will unite the staves with a straight bracket.
- The bar lines on the grand staff run continuously from the top staff to the bottom staff, while bar lines in an open score stop at the bottom of each staff. See **Ex. 1.1a** and **Ex. 1.1b**.
- In piano and instrumental music, consecutive flagged notes (eighth notes, sixteenth notes, etc.) within the same beat (or beat group) are beamed together. In choral music, flagged notes are only beamed together if they are part of a melisma (one syllable stretched over multiple notes) *and* within a beat structure.* See **Ex. 1.2a** and **Ex. 1.2b** for a comparison.

EX. 1.1a – Beethoven, Sonatina in G Major, Anh. 5, movt. II, mm. 1–8. Piano score, grand staff.

EX. 1.1a – continued

EX. 1.1b – Mozart, "Bei Männern welche Liebe fühlen," from *Die Zauberflöte*, mm. 11–13, open score.

The practice of breaking up metric beaming to indicate syllables may be changing. More and more contemporary scores and editions are applying the instrumental typography to choral scores as well. The metrical information provided by instrumental beaming is helpful for rhythmic reading, especially in complex contemporary music. This book will utilize the older typography because – although things are changing – most choral scores you will encounter still utilize the broken beam method.

EX. 1.2a – Mozart, "Bei Männern welche Liebe fühlen," from *Die Zauberflöte*, mm. 14–16, traditional beaming.

Note that the hand position changes on the second half of m.2.

EX. 1.2b – Mozart, "Bei Männern welche Liebe fühlen," from *Die Zauberflöte,* mm. 14–16, choral beaming.

As you can see from **Ex. 1.2b**, the lack of metric beaming can make a difference in a score's readability. It can be especially difficult with three or more staves involving complex rhythms, so it is very helpful to start with just two staves and accustom yourself to this format.

A final difference between open scores and piano music is the independence of voices. Music written for the piano often includes a relatively static, harmonic part in the bass clef while the treble clef contains a melodic line. Choral and instrumental music frequently includes more independence of voices, creating an added challenge when performing these voices at the piano. Exercises **1.3** and **1.4** are good examples of this – try both of them slowly at the piano after first looking over it.

EX. 1.3 – Diabelli, "Domine Exaudi," mm. 66–70.

EX. 1.4 – Purcell, "What Can We Poor Females Do," from *Orpheus Britannicus*, mm. 7–10.

EX. 1.4 – continued

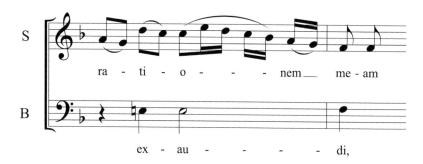

2 Sight-reading Exercises

Now that you know what to look for, try the following series of sight-reading exercises. For each exercise, you should first take 10–15 seconds to look over the exercise. During this time, do each of the following:

- Identify the key
- Identify the time signature
- Identify any accidentals
- Identify your hand position and write in fingerings where needed
- Choose a slow and careful tempo
- After you've looked over it, play all the way through the excerpt without stopping and at a steady tempo. Because this is sight-reading, resist the urge to stop and correct.

EX. 1.5 – Perosi, "Ave Verum," mm. 27–49.

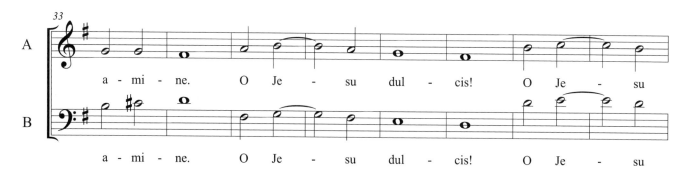

EX. 1.5 – continued

EX. 1.6 – Persichetti and Cummings, "Jimmie's Got a Goil," mm. 11–20.

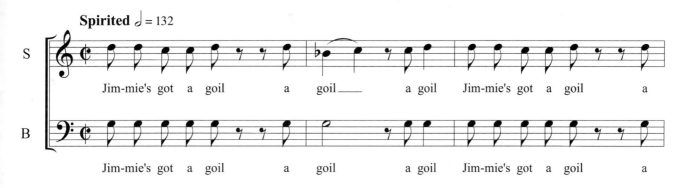

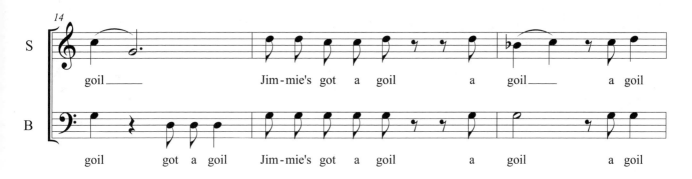

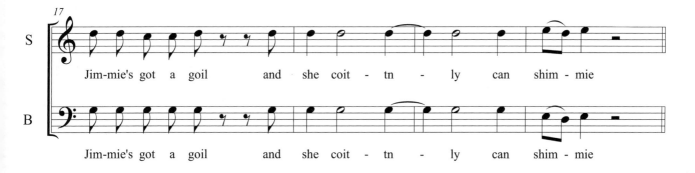

EX. 1.7 – Mozart, "Bei Männern welche Liebe fühlen," from *Die Zauberflöte,* mm. 11–17.

EX. 1.8 – Mendelssohn, "How Lovely Are the Messengers," mm. 10–18.

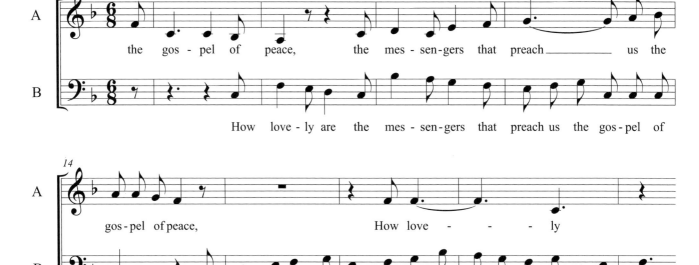

EX. 1.9 – Campian, "I Care Not for These Ladies."

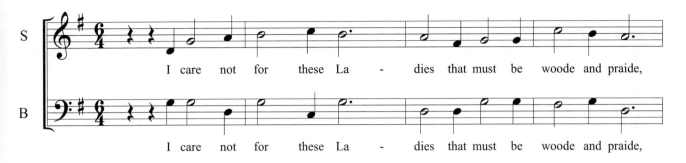

I care not for these La - dies that must be woode and praide,

I care not for these La - dies that must be woode and praide,

Na - ture art dis - dain - eth, her beau - tie is her owne, Her

Na - ture art dis - dain - eth, her beau - tie is her owne, Her

when __ we court and kisse, she creis __ for-sooth let go, but

when we court and kisse, she creis for-sooth let go, but

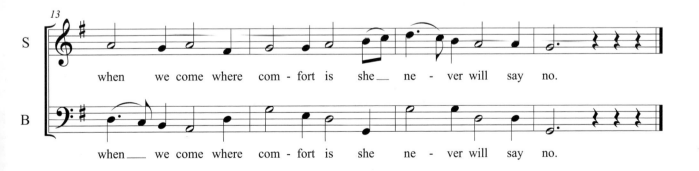

when we come where com - fort is she __ ne - ver will say no.

when __ we come where com - fort is she ne - ver will say no.

EX. 1.10 – Tarditi, "Inclina," mm. 1–24.

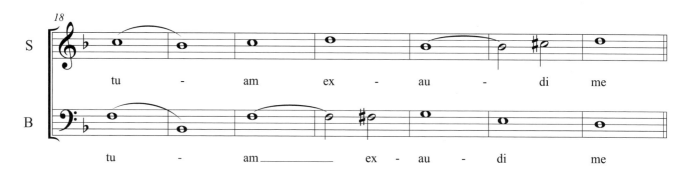

3 Prepared Exercises

For the following exercises, practice them over the course of a week. Feel free to mark fingerings, precautionary accidentals, or other markings that will aid in your performance.

EX. 1.11 – Handel, "The Righteous Shall Be Had," from *The Ways of Zion do Mourn*, mm. 48–63.

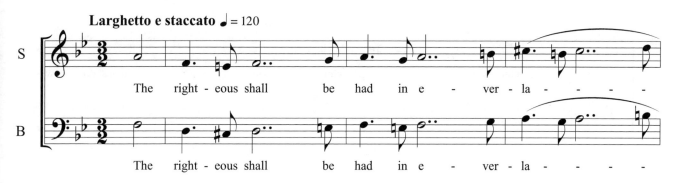

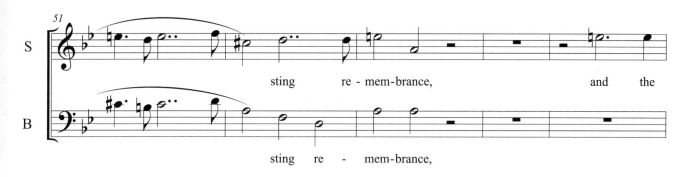

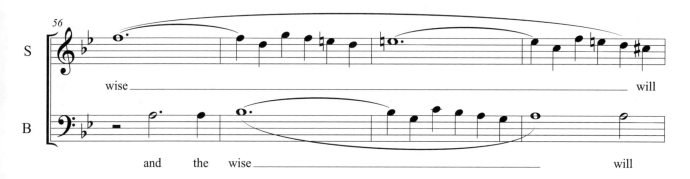

EX. 1.12 – Purcell, "What Can We Poor Females Do," from *Orpheus Britannicus*, mm. 1–10.

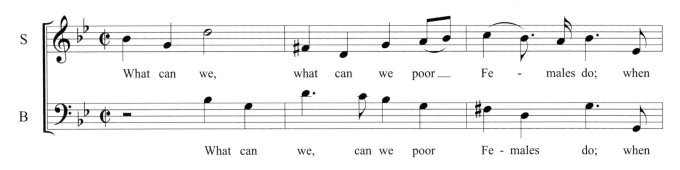

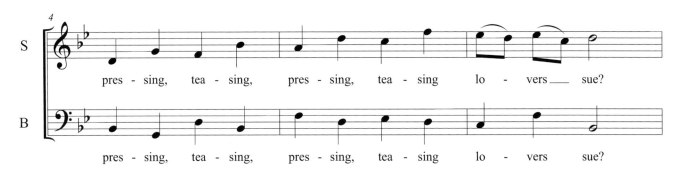

EX. 1.13 – Purcell, "For Love Ev'ry Creature Is Form'd," from *Orpheus Britannicus*, mm. 1–26.

EX. 1.14 – Dowland, "I Saw My Lady Weep," from *The Second Book of Songs or Ayres.*

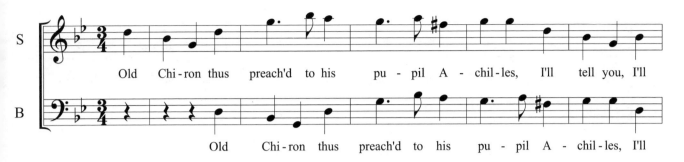

EX. 1.15 – Wise, "Old Chiron," mm. 1–34.

Two and Three Part Reading

EX. 1.15 − continued

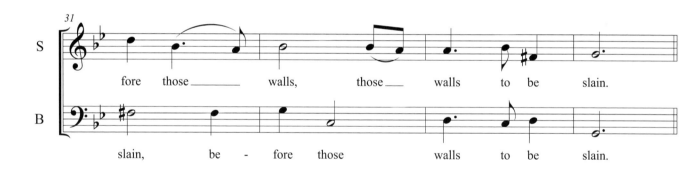

EX. 1.16 − Dowland, "Sorrow, Sorrow, Stay," mm. 1–24.

EX. 1.16 – continued

Chapter 2

Two Parts: Treble/ Treble and Bass/Bass

1 Introduction

While reading two-part scores with treble and bass clefs is very similar to reading from a grand staff, reading from two treble or two bass clefs adds a new wrinkle to score reading. Although visually removed from each other (**Ex. 2.1a**), two parts in the same clef will frequently be very close on the keyboard (**Ex. 2.1b**).

EX. 2.1a – Mendelssohn, "Abendlied," mm. 6–9.

EX. 2.1b – Mendelssohn, "Abendlied," mm. 6–9, single staff reduction.

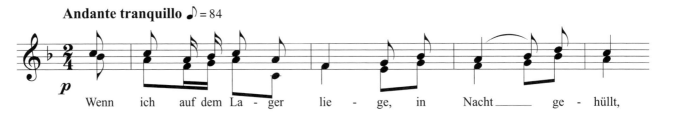

Through practice, a pianist can become accustomed to reading in this format, and develop techniques to deal with close spacings and the occasional crossed parts that can also occur. In most cases, you will want to use both hands when reading two-part scores, but you should feel free to use one hand if it is more convenient or if you would like to conduct with the other hand.

2 Intervallic Notations

One of the most helpful habits an open score reader can develop is the use of intervallic notations. Reading multiple staves, especially with leaping parts, can make recognition of harmonic intervals difficult, so it is important to visually indicate intervallic landmarks. For example, on the downbeat of m. 2 in **Ex. 2.1a**, the soprano and alto parts move in contrary motion to a unison. Playing an unexpected unison can surprise and confuse the best pianist, and so identifying such intervals during a cursory score analysis can be very helpful. Developing a shorthand for indicating intervals allows you to quickly and recognizably identify such landmarks and avoid being surprised when you encounter them later. In **Ex. 2.1c** below, an indication has been written in to warn that the two parts will be in unison.*

EX. 2.1c – Mendelssohn, "Abendlied," mm. 6–9, with unison indicated.

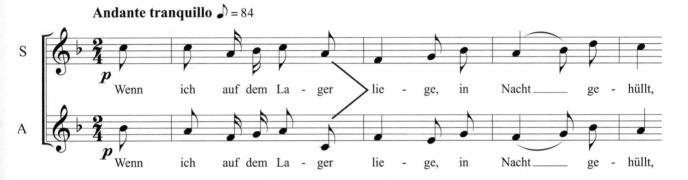

The indications in this text are suggestions. Pianists frequently develop their own shorthand for intervallic indications, and you should feel free to use whatever symbols are most convenient for you. The important thing is to remain consistent in your use so that your eyes quickly recognize the symbols you have indicated.

Try playing through the following excerpt and note any areas of difficulty.

EX. 2.2a – Brahms, *Neue Liebeslieder*, No. 13, mm. 7–10.

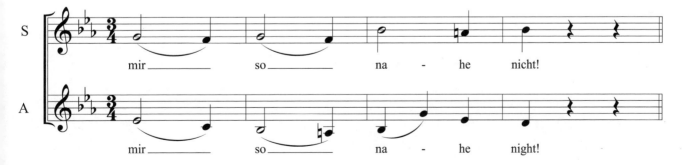

Did the downbeat of m. 9 cause any problems? Octaves in an open score can surprise a pianist due to the sudden consonance and apparent loss of one of the voices. In the following example, an indication has been included to warn of the octave—play through the example and see if the indication is helpful.

EX. 2.2b – Brahms, *Neue Liebeslieder*, No. 13, mm. 7–10, with octave indicated.

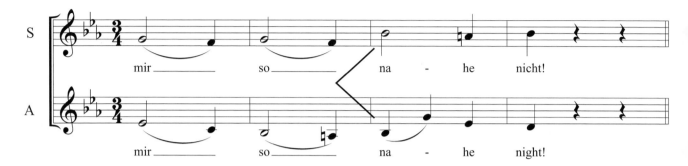

Parallel Thirds and Sixths

Parallel thirds and sixths are also excellent landmarks to identify as you prepare a score. As the most common intervals, a long chain (usually more than three or four consecutive occurrences) of thirds or sixths is helpful to identify. In **Ex. 2.3** the successive thirds are identified with a long horizontal line with a "3" on it.

EX. 2.3 – Dering, "Gaudent in Coelis," mm. 14–18.

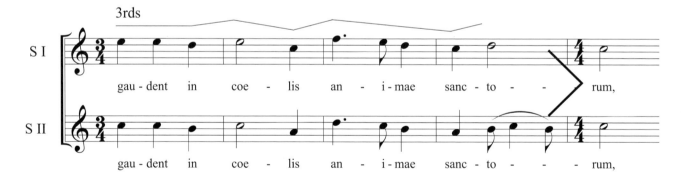

Before performing this example mark all places in the score where the voices move in parallel motion. *Note the brief occurrences of fourths.*

EX. 2.4 – Purcell, "We the Spirits of the Air," mm. 1–8.

Finally, voice crossings can disrupt a performance if the pianist is not aware they are approaching. A brief score analysis before playing can allow the pianist to identify and label these crossings and avoid an unwelcome surprise. Try playing **Ex. 2.5a** without first looking over the excerpt.

EX. 2.5a – Fauré, "Madrigal," mm. 36–39.

Now perform **Ex. 2.5b**—the same excerpt with an indication for the voice crossing. Was this helpful?

EX. 2.5b – Fauré, "Madrigal," mm. 36–39, with crossing indication.

Playing Bass/Bass Open Scores

In addition to encountering treble/treble writing, you may also encounter bass/bass writing excerpts, either as a duet or as part of a larger ensemble. **Ex. 2.6** gives you a good introduction to this scoring. Feel free to write in intervallic indications—this excerpt includes thirds, sixths, octaves and unisons.

EX. 2.6 – Bruckner, "Os Justi," mm. 9–16, bass parts excerpted.

EX. 2.7 – Elgar, "There is Sweet Music," Op. 53, No.1, mm. 26–32, bass parts excerpted.

EX. 2.7 – continued

For more accomplished pianists, writing in intervallic indications for two-part scores may seem unnecessary, but the technique becomes increasingly valuable as you add voices and complexity to your open scores. Therefore it is advisable that you develop the habit of indicating landmark intervals in simpler scores, so that your recognition of, and familiarity with the symbols is well-engrained by the time you really need them.

3 Sight-reading Exercises

For all of the following sight-reading exercises, quickly look over the scores before playing them in order to identify landmark intervals (octaves, unisons, parallel thirds and sixths). Note that fingerings are not given. Because you will not find fingerings indicated in "real" open scores, the authors have omitted them in all of the following excerpts. As was suggested in the last chapter, you should look over each excerpt before playing it to identify the proper hand position and possible fingering challenges.

EX. 2.8 – Morley, "Sweet Nymph Come to Thy Lover," mm. 1–5.

EX. 2.9 – Saint-Saens, *Ave Maria*, mm. 2–19.

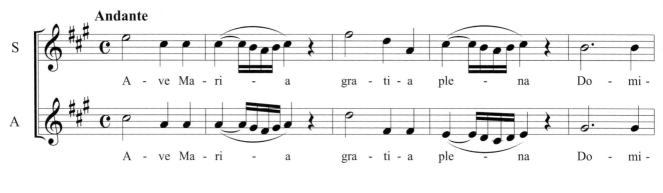

EX. 2.10 – Dvořák, "The Dove and the Maple Tree," Op. 31, No. 1, mm. 3–26.

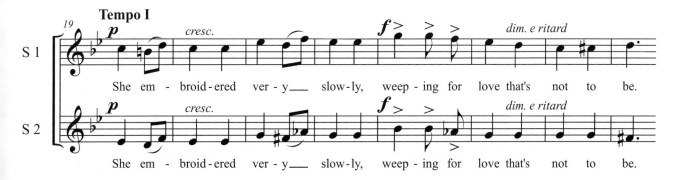

EX. 2.11 – Schubert, "Grüner wird die Au," from *Fünf Duette*, D. 199.

EX. 2.12 – Brahms, "Nachtwache, No. 1," Op.104a, mm. 10–19, bass parts excerpted.

EX. 2.12 – continued

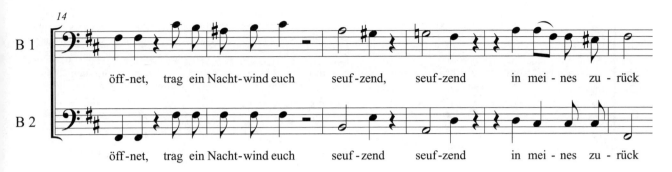

Watch out for the voice crossings in the following examples. Indicate where the crossings begin and end to aid in your performance. Because of the close spacing and voice-crossing it may be easier to perform all or most of the excerpt with just one hand. Mark in fingerings to facilitate your chosen format.

EX. 2.13 – Fauré, "Madrigal," mm. 23–39.

EX. 2.14 – Dering, *Gaudent in Coelis*, mm. 27–32.

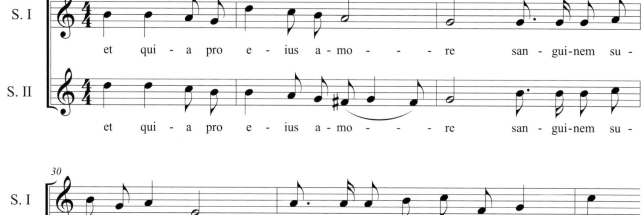

The following example is lengthier than most sight-reading examples, but is comprised of primarily thirds. Identify the instances in which the two voices are NOT thirds before playing.

EX. 2.15 – Grieg, "Arabisk dans," from *Peer Gynt*, mm. 21–45.

EX. 2.15 – continued

4 Prepared Exercises

The following exercises are to be prepared over the course of several days or a week. Again, utilize intervallic indications to speed the learning process.

EX. 2.16 – Schumann, "Mailied," Op. 79, No. 10, mm. 1–35

EX. 2.16 – continued

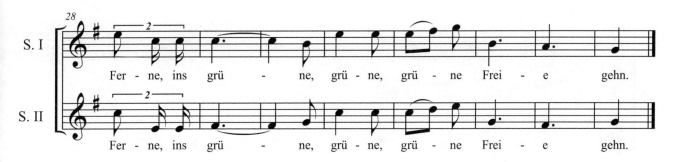

EX. 2.17 – Brahms, "Nein, Geliebter, setze dich," from *Neue Liebeslieder*, mm. 3–25.

EX. 2.17 – continued

EX. 2.18 – Lotti, *Crucifixus*, mm. 1–11, bass parts excerpted.

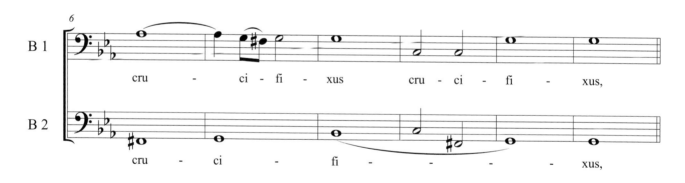

For the following two excerpts (**Ex. 2.19** and **Ex. 2.20**) contemporary, metric beaming is used. Many pianists will find this simplifies learning and reading the open scores.

EX. 2.19 – Spiritual, Arr. by Shaw, "This Train," mm. 27–42.

EX. 2.20 – Grey, "The Clouds," mm. 29–44.

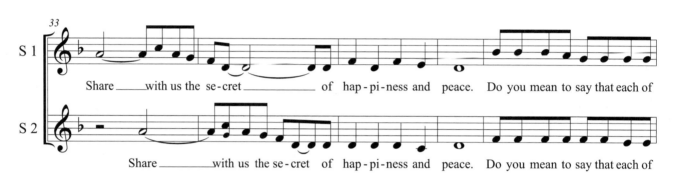

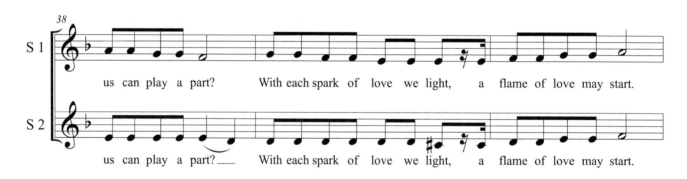

Because of the close spacing and voice crossing, feel free to either play both parts with one hand, or cross your hands when the soprano 2 moves above soprano 1.

EX. 2.21 – Gabrieli, "Diligam Te, Domine," mm. 5–22, bass parts excerpted.

Chapter 3

Three Parts: Treble/Treble/Bass

_____

1 Introduction

Now that you are comfortable playing two parts with the treble and bass clef, you are ready to move on to three-part reading that includes both treble and bass clefs. In this chapter you will work with SAB writing. In general you should perform the soprano and alto parts with the right hand and the bass parts with the left hand.

Parallel Thirds

It is important to note that soprano and alto parts frequently move in parallel thirds and sixths. Being able to quickly identify instances of parallel motion will improve your open score sight-reading ability. In **Ex. 3.1**, the soprano and alto are entirely in thirds—note the suggested fingering and play through the example. When consecutive thirds move out of a five-finger position, it is frequently helpful to extend the thumb, as in m. 44 and m. 48.

EX. 3.1 – Gounod, "O Salutaris Hostia," from *Seven Motets*, mm. 41–49.

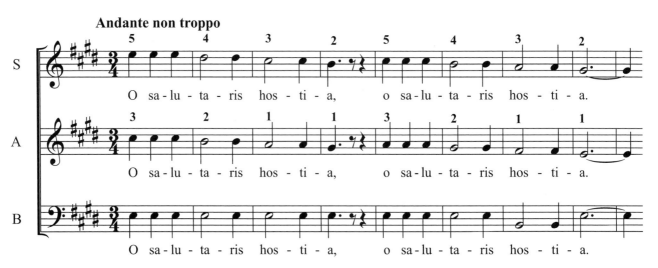

In the next two examples the soprano and alto parts move mainly in parallel thirds. Keep in mind the fingering suggestions from **Ex. 3.1**, making use of thumb extensions when needed.

- Before playing, look over the score and circle the one beat on which the soprano and alto are NOT in parallel thirds.
- A few fingering suggestions have been placed in the score. Be sure to determine an effective fingering pattern for the entire right and left hand parts before performing the excerpt with both hands.

EX. 3.2 – Thomas Morley, *O Fly Not, Love*, mm. 1–7.

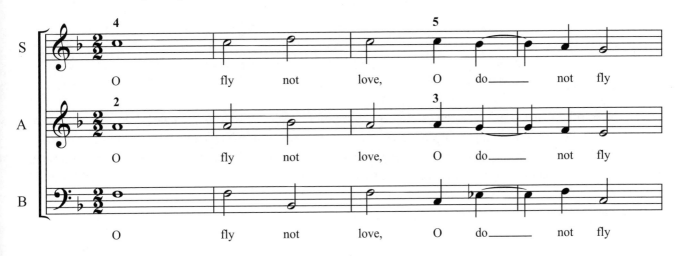

Parallel Sixths

While parallel sixths are as common as parallel thirds, fingering them can be more difficult because of the greater reach. When found in the right hand, it is usually most effective to "hop" your thumb from sixth to sixth in the alto part while using 5, 4 and 3 for the soprano part. **Ex. 3.3** illustrates this fingering technique.

EX. 3.3 – Haydn, *Maker of All! Psalm 41*, mm. 59–62.

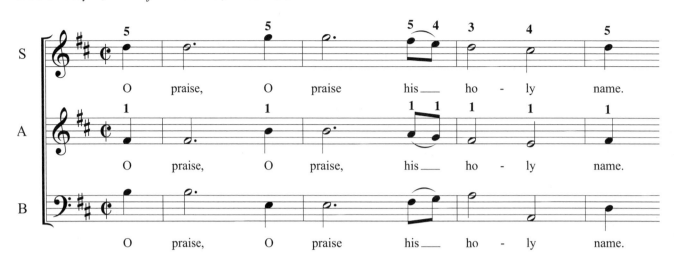

In the following example the parallel sixths are more extensive. Although a variety of fingerings can be used, the authors suggest the one indicated, as it allows for a legato melody line. It should be noted that pianists with larger hands may prefer using a series of 4–1, 5–2 fingerings, while pianists with relaxed wrist technique might choose consecutive 5–1 fingerings.

EX. 3.4 – Redner, *Oh Little Town of Bethlehem*, arr. by S. Gregorich mm. 1–4.

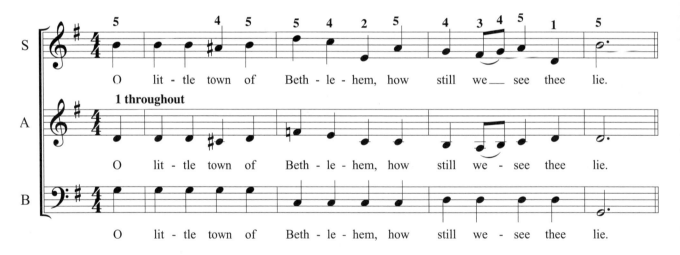

For the next example, be sure to have a plan for fingering the thirds in the dotted passages. Delays in the midst of a dotted rhythm significantly compromise rehearsal effectiveness, and these can be avoided by looking over the score and choosing a fingering. We have included fingerings in one of the problem spots; be sure to address the other spots before playing.

EX. 3.5 – Traditional, *Come, Come Ye Saints*, mm. 1–4.

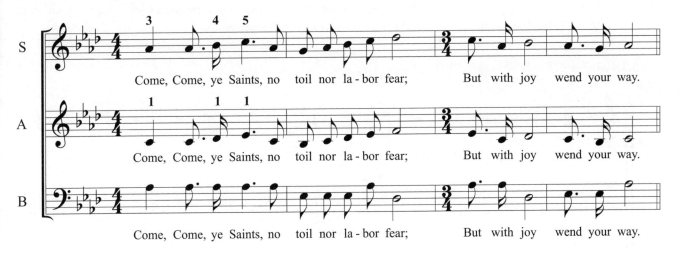

Wide Reaches

Soprano and alto parts usually lie within an octave of one another, but in **Ex. 3.6** the soprano and alto parts are a tenth apart in two places. Note that this occurs when one voice remains static and the other part moves by leap. When this occurs the alto part may be played by the left hand, thereby temporarily redistributing the parts between the hands.

EX. 3.6 – Mozart, "Ecco quel fiero istante," KV 436.

In this example the soprano and alto are separated by a tenth in m. 5. The alto D could be played by the left hand and the bass note omitted. Since the omitted bass note is a repetition of the previous bass note in m. 4, the basses should not need the piano support for this note.

EX. 3.7 – Mozart, "Píu non si trovano," KV 549, mm. 1-8.

2 Sight-reading Exercises

All orchestral parts, including the two measure introduction, have been omitted in order to focus on reading the vocal parts.

EX. 3.8 – Diabelli, *Gradualia*, mm. 3–14.

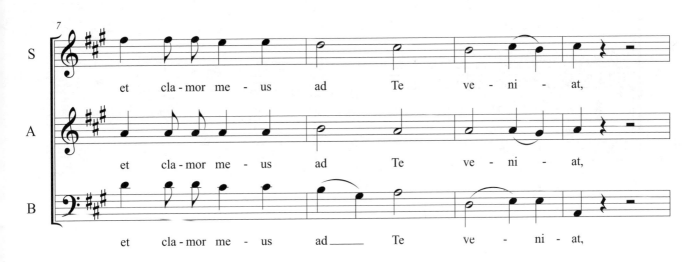

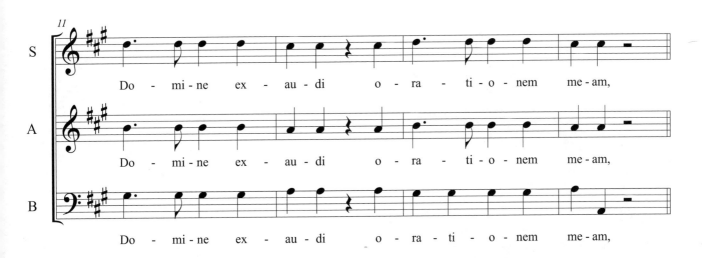

In this example indicate where the soprano and alto parts create thirds and sixths.

EX. 3.9 – Haydn, *Maker of All!* Psalm 41, mm. 48–56.

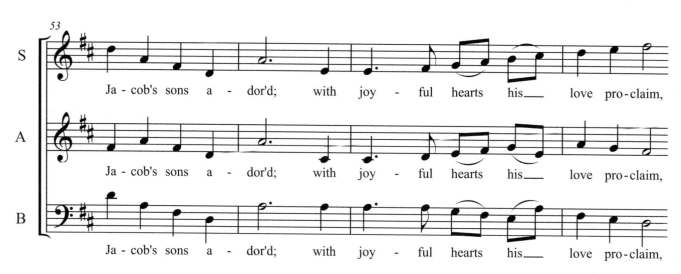

EX. 3.10 – Lotti, "Kyrie," from *Mass in Three Voices in La Minor*, arr. for SAB, mm. 1–18.

Notice the rest on beat 3, m.2. This is an excellent place to turn the page for the remainder of the excerpt.

The soprano and alto in this exercise diverge from parallel thirds when one part remains static while the other moves. At the end, note the inversion of thirds, creating parallel sixths.

EX. 3.11 – Mozart, "Luci care, luci belle," KV 346, mm. 1–8.

S: Lu - ci ca - re, lu - ci bel - le, ca - ri
A: Lu - ci ca - re, lu - ci bel - le, ca - ri
B: Lu - ci ca - re, lu - ci bel - le, ca - ri

S: lu - mi, a - ma - te stel - le, da - te cal - ma_a que - sto
A: lu - mi, a - ma - te stel - le, da - te cal - ma_a que - sto
B: lu - mi, ma - te stel - le, da - te cal - ma_a que - sto

S: co - re, da - te cal - ma a que - sto cor - re!
A: co - re, da - te cal - ma a que - sto cor - re!
B: co - re, da - te cal - ma que - sto cor - re!

3 Prepared Exercises

The following exercises should be self-prepared. When preparing open scores, feel free to mark your score with indications that will facilitate your performance of the work. Writing in fingering patterns, intervallic relationships and cautionary accidentals can help speed the preparation process.

- In this example there are three instances where the soprano and alto parts are not in parallel thirds. Circle these spots and write in a fingering to facilitate this shift.
- Measures 7 and 8 present a tricky fingering pattern. Although one fingering solution has been presented, you may want to experiment with other options to find a pattern that is comfortable for you.

EX. 3.12 – Mozart, "Due pupille amabili," KV 439, mm. 1–12.

Occasionally the soprano and alto parts will cross one another. Visually identify these crossings and mark the occurrence in the score before playing.

EX. 3.13 – Haydn, *Maker of All!* Psalm 41, mm. 7–21.

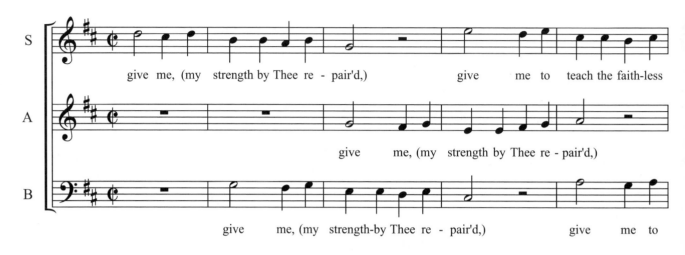

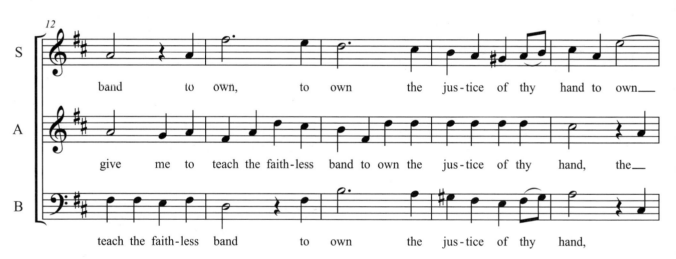

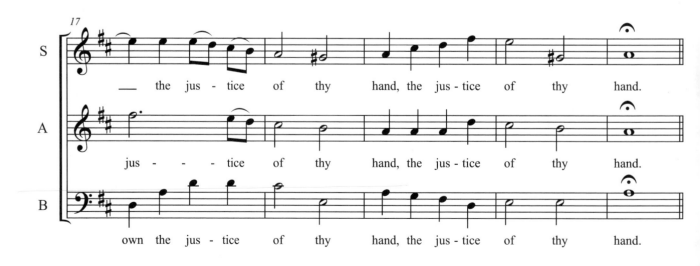

EX. 3.14 – Holborne, *Change Then, for Lo She Changeth*, mm. 1–14.

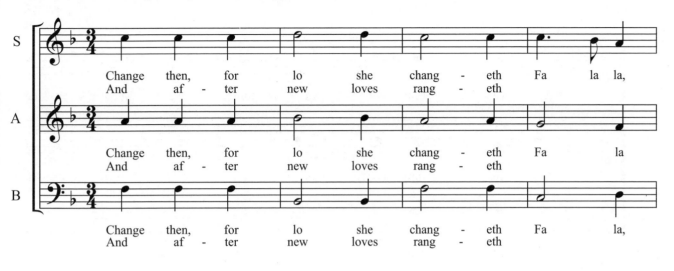

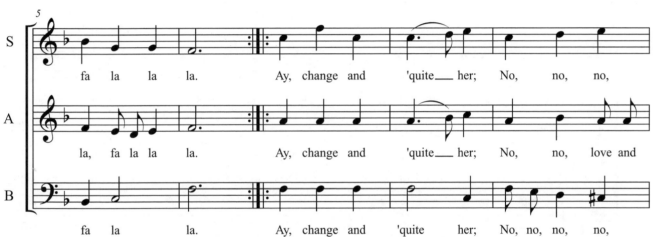

EX. 3.15 – Gounod, "Ave Verum," from *Seven Motets*, mm. 1–16.

EX. 3.16 – Traditional, arr. Covin, "Liza Jane," mm. 7–14.

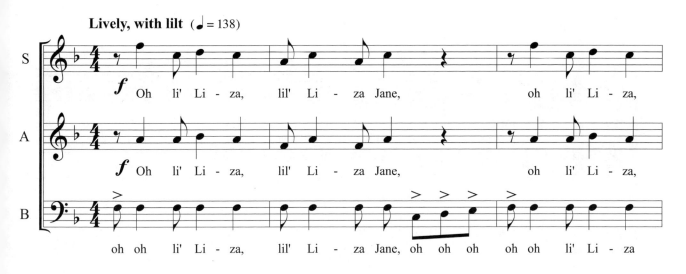

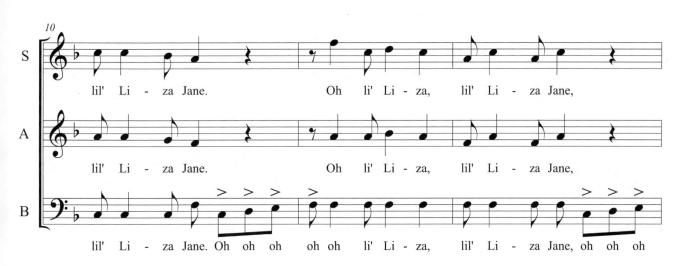

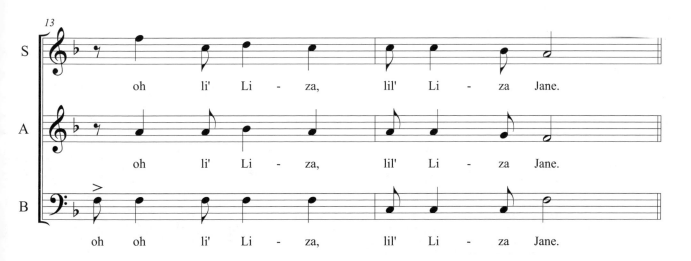

Note the crossings between the soprano and alto parts.

EX. 3.17 – Locke, *Ne'er Trouble Thyself*, mm. 1–16.

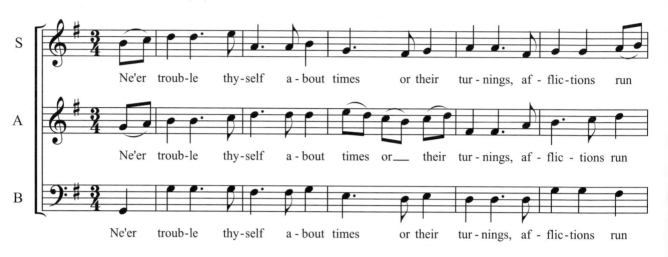

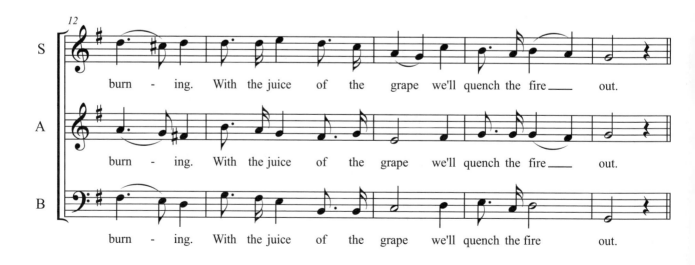

This example has a more contrapuntal texture than other examples in this chapter, although much of the counterpoint elaborates a texture that still emphasizes parallel thirds and sixths. In m.6 how can you redistribute the points in order to accommodate the interval of a tenth between the soprano and alto parts?

EX. 3.18 – Gounod, "Da Pacem," from *Seven Motets*, mm. 1–13.

Chapter 4

Three Parts: All Treble

1 Introduction

Three-part treble clef scores are fairly common in both the instrumental and vocal repertoire. Women's choruses and boys' choruses frequently use soprano I – soprano II – alto scoring; many of the following exercises are excerpts from these ensembles. Although an open score using only one clef may seem simple, many pianists find the lack of a bass clef in the bottom system confusing. Additional challenges include the close proximity of the three parts, the resulting voice crossings, and frequent unisons that may surprise the pianist.

Before playing any three-part open score, it is always helpful to quickly look over the score and decide which hands will play which parts. Look over **Ex. 4.1**—which distribution of voices between the hands might you choose?

EX. 4.1 – Gounod, "Da Pacem," mm. 1–8.

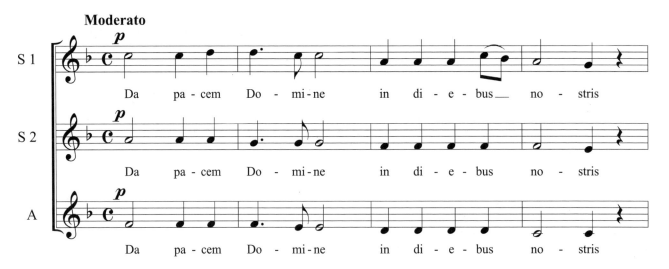

EX. 4.1 – continued

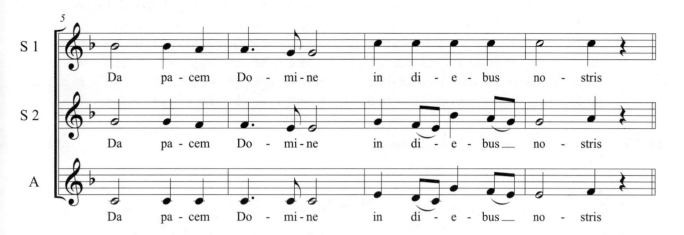

Although grouping either S1–S2 / A or S1 / S2–A would work, the rhythmic similarities between the alto and soprano II in measure 7 would suggest the latter grouping. If spacing between the parts is not an issue, similar rhythms should determine how you split the parts between the hands. How would you distribute the parts in **Ex. 4.2**? Write in a bracket to group the parts you will play with the same hand.

EX. 4.2 – Wood, "Music When Soft Voices Die," mm. 8–15.

In the previous examples it was possible to identify a voice distribution that would work consistently throughout the excerpt. Sometimes an excerpt may not lend itself to one distribution throughout and you may need to switch. Use the techniques of grouping like rhythmic patterns together in the following example to choose your voice distributions. You may want to switch from one distribution to another at various points throughout the excerpt. Once you have determined appropriate distributions, identify proper fingerings and write these in the score. Unlike Chapter 3 where some fingerings were provided, the following chapters provide you with the opportunity to develop this skill on your own.

EX. 4.3 – Fauré, "Tantum Ergo," Op. 65, No. 2, mm. 2–7.

Another clue that can help you choose the best voice distribution is the presence of parallel thirds. A chain of parallel thirds between two adjacent voices can indicate that these voices should be paired in the same hand. Look over **Exs. 4.4–4.6** and mark in the parallel thirds. Then choose a voice distribution that places the thirds in the same hand.

EX. 4.4 – Baini, "Panis Angelicus," mm. 1–11.

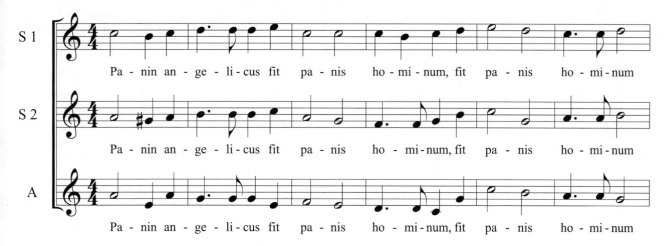

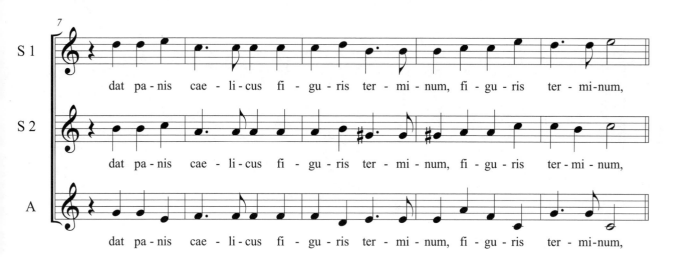

EX. 4.5 – Stanford, "Beati Quorum Via," mm. 1–9, SSA excerpted.

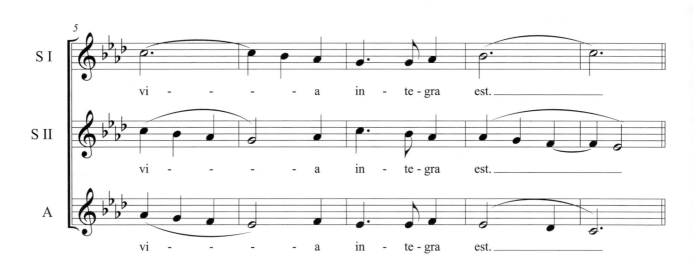

EX. 4.6 – Vaughan Williams, "Sound Sleep," mm. 82–85.

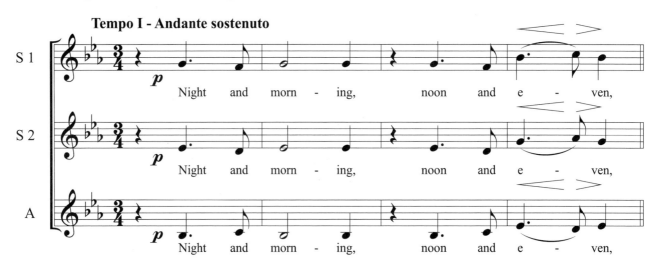

In addition to thirds, you should also be used to dealing with unisons by this point, although in three part treble open scores, you may encounter more than you're used to. Marking out the notes that double (or triple) other parts will be helpful. See **Ex. 4.7** for an example of this.

EX. 4.7 – Arr. by Hayes, "Go Down Moses," mm. 45–52.

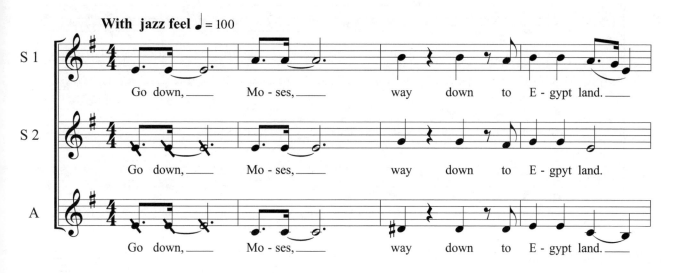

When marking out unisons, be careful of *which* unison you mark out. Compare the two versions of **Ex. 4.8** below, given the voice distribution indicated. Which is easier to play?

EX. 4.8a – Grieg, "Ved Rundarne," mm. 3–5.

EX. 4.8b – Grieg, "Ved Rundarne," mm. 3–5.

2 Sight-reading Exercises

For the following excerpts, quickly look over the material before playing it straight through. Feel free to make a few marks, including indications of voice crossings, parallel thirds and sixths, unisons and the distribution of voices between the hands.

EX. 4.9 – Schubert, "Wer wird Zähren sanften Mitlieds," from *Stabat Mater*, mm. 26–33. Scored for SATB divisi. S1, S2, and A excerpted.

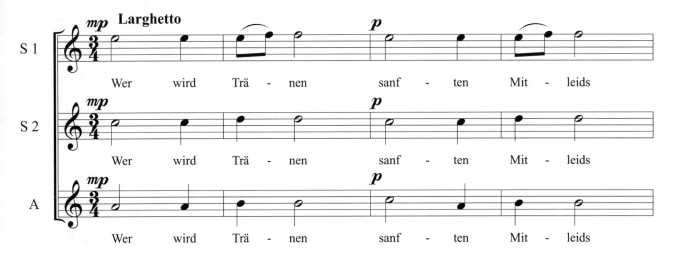

EX. 4.10 – Mendelssohn, "Die Engel," from *Elijah*, mm. 1–8.

For the following exercise, notice the static soprano II part. How can you use this to your advantage?

EX. 4.11 – Vaughan Williams, "Sound Sleep," mm. 12–17.

EX. 4.12 – Gounod, "Da Pacem," mm. 9–20.

EX. 4.13 – Schumann, *Requiem für Mignon*, No. 5, Op. 98b, mm. 252–267.

Although this movement is scored for SAB, the excerpt below contains a solo for soprano divisi and alto. Notated here on three staves.

Notice that the alto part drops out for a measure in **Ex. 4.14**. Because it is easier to separate the two soprano parts between the hands at that point, try performing the whole excerpt with soprano II and alto in the LH, and soprano I in the RH.

EX. 4.14 – Schubert, "Coronach," mm. 5–8.

Watch for the voice crossings in the following excerpt. It can be helpful to write in "V.C." where the voices cross.

EX. 4.15 – Baini, "Panis Angelicus," mm. 12–15.

3 Prepared Exercises

The following excerpts should be practiced over the course of several days or a week. While you might write in just a few indications for sight-reading excerpts, feel free to use more extensive indications for these, including fingerings, parallel intervals, and voice crossings.

EX. 4.16 – Traditional, lyrics by Samuel Francis Smith, "My Country 'Tis of Thee," mm. 1–14.*

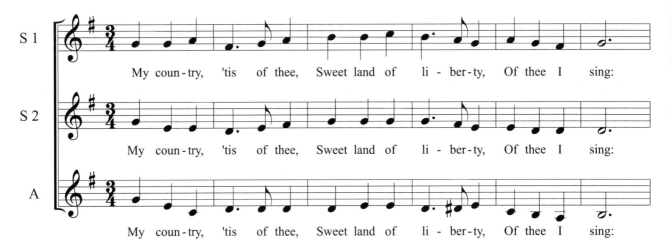

EX. 4.16 – continued

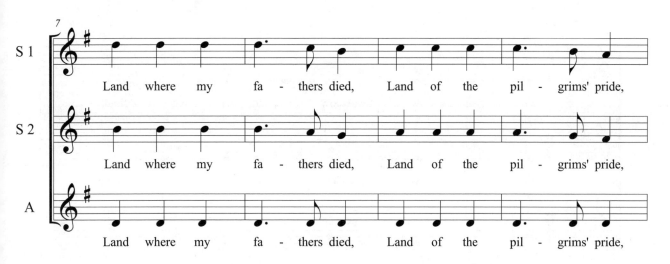

S 1: Land where my fa - thers died, Land of the pil - grims' pride,

S 2: Land where my fa - thers died, Land of the pil - grims' pride,

A: Land where my fa - thers died, Land of the pil - grims' pride,

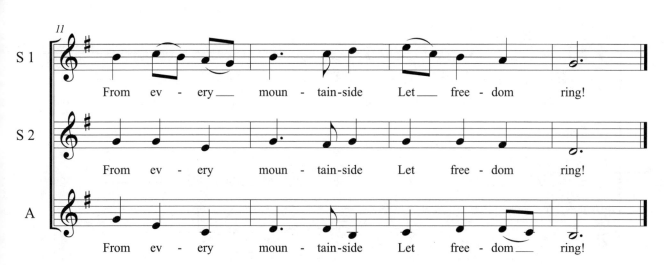

S 1: From ev - ery __ moun - tain-side Let __ free - dom ring!

S 2: From ev - ery moun - tain-side Let free - dom ring!

A: From ev - ery moun - tain-side Let free - dom __ ring!

* The melody comes from the British national anthem, "God Save the Queen." The origins of this piece are unknown, although some musicologists have pointed out the similarities between it and several traditional English plainsongs of the fifteenth and sixteenth centuries. Given the British origins of the piece, there is considerable irony that Smith's song was first performed for an American Independence Day celebration.

EX. 4.17 – Holst, "Oh Swallow, Swallow," mm. 1–9.

EX. 4.18 – Grieg, "Ved Rundarne," mm. 5–17.

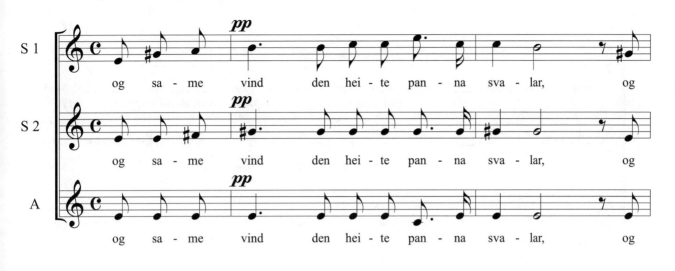

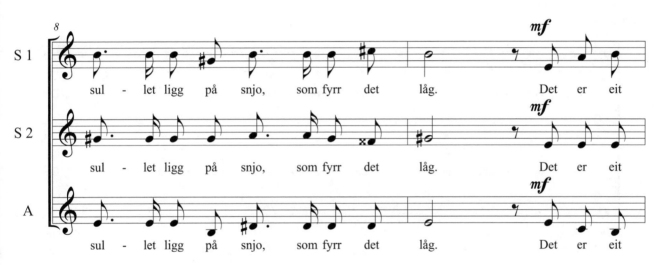

EX. 4.18 – continued

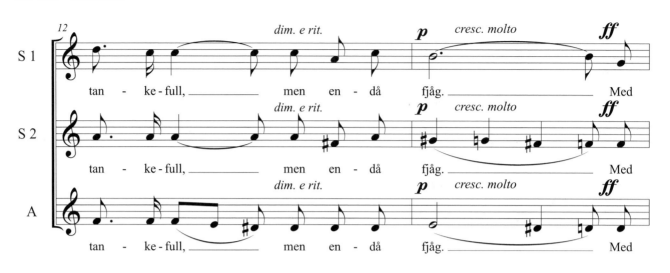

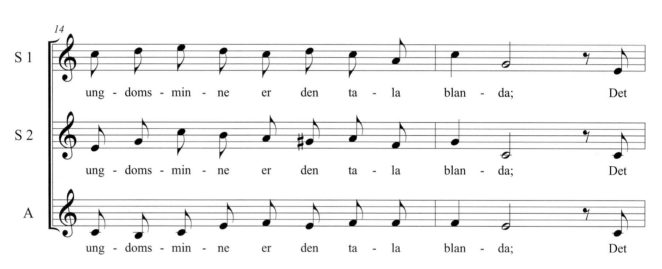

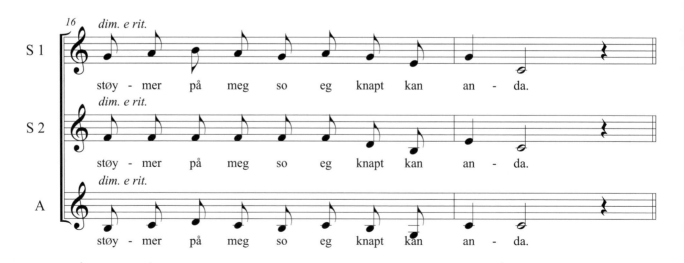

EX. 4.19 – Thompson, "A Girl's Garden," from *Frostiana*, mm. 76–82.

EX. 4.20 – Grieg, "Sporven," mm. 3–22.

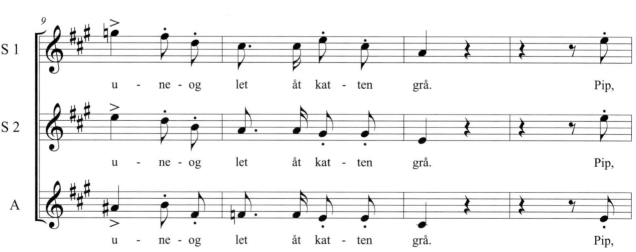

EX. 4.20 – continued

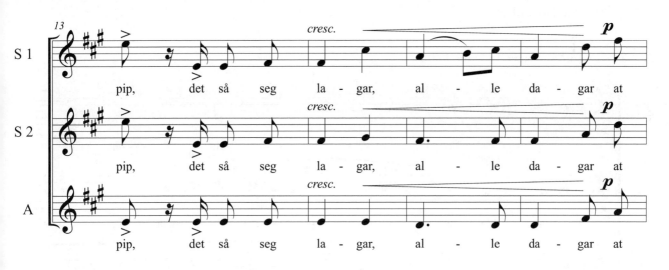

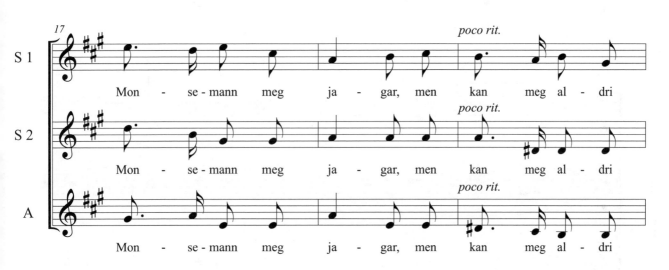

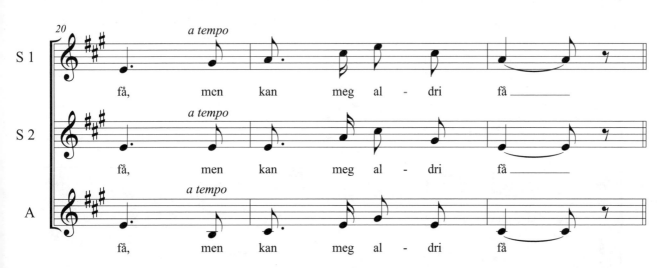

Look out for the voice crossing in m. 3 of **Ex. 4.20**. Note where the crossings begin, and where they return to standard order.

EX. 4.21 – Lasso, "Adoramus Te," mm. 1–10.

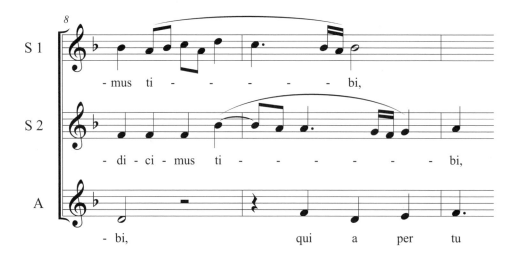

Part 2

Two and Three Part Reading including the Tenor

Chapter 5

Two Parts: Treble/Tenor and Tenor/Bass

---

1 Introduction

Tenor parts are unique amongst choral parts in that they require a transposition. Although written in the treble clef, they are sung an octave below. For many pianists, this may be their first exposure to playing a transposing part, so in this chapter you will find tips and suggestions to help you develop this new skill.

It is important to remember that tenor parts written in the treble clef *always* transpose down an octave. Some scores will use a standard treble clef, while other scores will use a treble clef with a small "8" beneath (see **Ex. 5.1a** and **Ex. 5.1b**). This clef is sometimes called an "octave-dropped" treble clef, or sometimes a "tenor clef."* Regardless of which treble clef an editor chooses to use, the tenor part still transposes down an octave. The only exception would be if an editor scored the tenor part in the bass clef, in which case it would be sung as written (**Ex. 5.1c**).

The following three excerpts all indicate the exact same pitches.

EX. 5.1a – Traditional, "Yankee Doodle," mm. 1–4, using a treble clef.

EX. 5.1b – Traditional, "Yankee Doodle," mm. 1–4, using an octave-dropped treble clef.

EX. 5.1c – Traditional, "Yankee Doodle," mm. 1–4, using a bass clef.

Yan - kee Doo - dle   went to town,   ri - ding on a po - ny,

It is best to avoid describing the octave-dropped treble clef as a "tenor clef." A true tenor clef is a C-clef placed on the fourth line of the staff and is most often found in cello, bassoon, euphonium, trombone and double bass scores. Older choral scores may use the tenor clef for tenor parts, but it is gradually falling out of use.

As in previous chapters, it can be helpful to identify parallel motion when working with tenor parts. Be aware, however, that due to the octave transposition, what looks like parallel thirds will sound as parallel tenths or sixths. See **Ex. 5.2–Ex. 5.4** for examples.

EX. 5.2 – Handel, "Wash Me Thoroughly," from *Chandos Anthem, No. 3*, mm. 47–54.

EX. 5.3 – Handel, "The Righteous Shall Be Had," from *The Ways of Zion Do Mourn*, mm. 25–30.

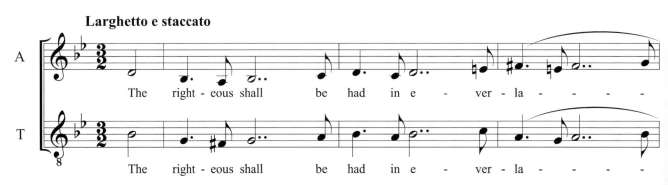

EX. 5.3 – continued

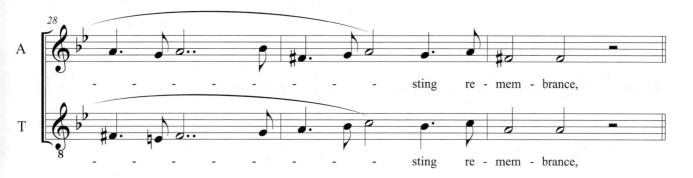

EX. 5.4 – Traditional, "Deck the Halls," mm. 1–4.

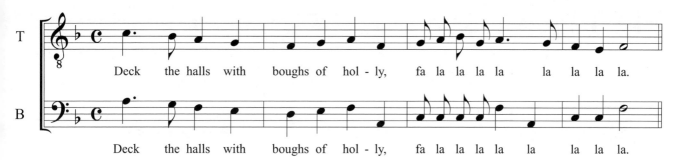

You will also encounter occasional octaves. In the first line of the following excerpt the brackets indicate where the octaves begin and where the two parts diverge. Do the same for the second phrase.

EX. 5.5 – Traditional, arr. Gregorich, "All Through the Night," mm. 1–8.

Because of the transposition, it will be helpful to indicate where unisons occur, since they may surprise you in performance. Writing in intervallic landmarks also provides checkpoints to improve your confidence as you play the open score. In **Ex. 5.6** the simultaneous unisons, and unisons separated by a beat have been indicated for you.

EX. 5.6 – Thompson, "Say Ye to the Righteous," from *The Peaceable Kingdom*, mm. 1–8.

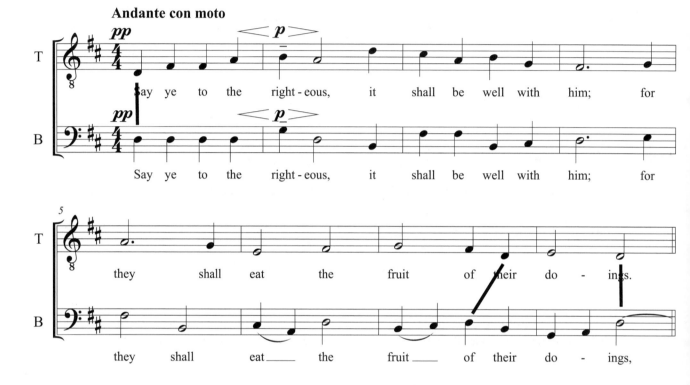

2 Sight-reading Exercises

Before performing each example scan the score for instances of parallel motion, unisons, imitation, or anything that may be of assistance to you.

EX. 5.7 – Charpentier, "Pour la Vierge," mm. 1–7.

EX. 5.8 – Brahms, "O die Frauen," Op. 52, No. 3, mm. 1–8.

EX. 5.9 – Fauré, "Maria, mater gratiae," Op. 47, No. 2, mm. 41–52.

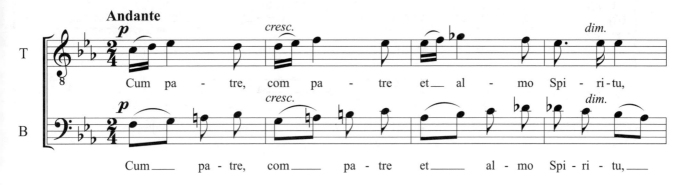

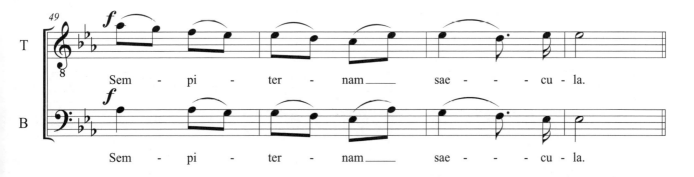

EX. 5.10 – Brahms, "Sieh', wie ist die Welle klar," mm. 1–16.

EX. 5.11 – Schumann, "Wiegenlied," from *Vier Duette*, mm. 2–32.

EX. 5.12 – Skuhersky, "Kyrie," from *Missa a duas voces aequales*, mm. 41–50.

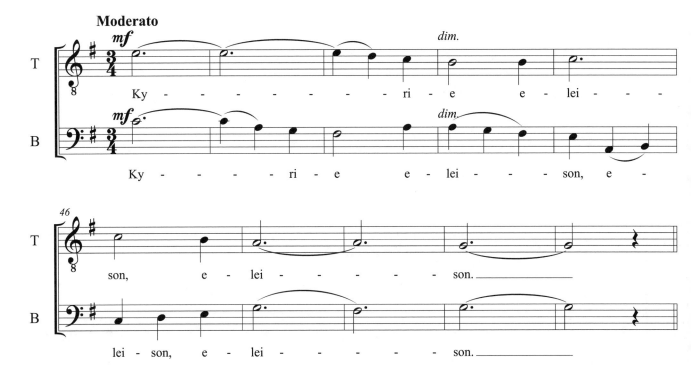

EX. 5.13 – Handel, "Wash Me Thoroughly," from *Chandos Anthem No. 3*, mm. 38–46. Note the imitation in the following excerpt.

EX. 5.14 – Fauré, "Madrigal," mm. 75–83.

3 Prepared Exercises

The following excerpts should be practiced over the course of several days or a week. While you might write in just a few indications for sight-reading excerpts, feel free to use more extensive indications for these, including fingerings, parallel intervals, and imitation.

EX. 5.15 – Haydn, "Credo," from *Paukenmesse*, mm. 3–8, tenor and bass excerpted.

EX. 5.16 – Mendelssohn, "My Song Shall Be Always Thy Mercy," mm. 35–45.

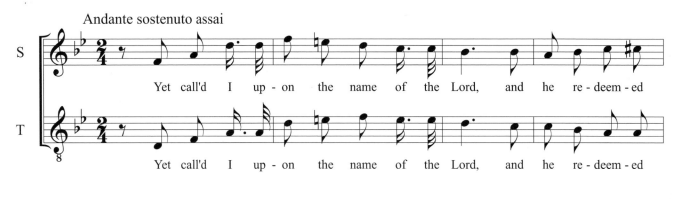

EX. 5.17 – Schumann, "So wahr die Sonne scheinet," mm. 1–36.

EX. 5.17 – continued

S: wahr die Flam-me sprüht, so wahr der Frü-ling blüht, so wahr hab ich emp-

T: wahr die Flam-me sprüht, so wahr der Frü-ling blüht, so wahr hab ich emp-

S: fun - den, wie ich dich halt um-wun - den; du liebst mich wie ich

T: fun - den, wie ich dich halt um - wun - den; du liebst mich wie ich

S: dich, dich lieb ich wie du___ mich. Die Son - ne mag ver -

T: dich, dich lieb ich wie du___ mich. Die Son - ne mag ver -

S: schei - nen, die Wol - ke nicht mehr wei - nen, die Flam - me mag ver -

T: schei - nen, die Wol - ke nicht mehr wei - nen, die Flam - me mag ver -

EX. 5.17 – continued

sprühn,   der Früh - ling nicht mehr blühn: wir   wol - len uns um -

sprühn,   der Früh - ling nicht mehr blühn: wir   wol - len uns um -

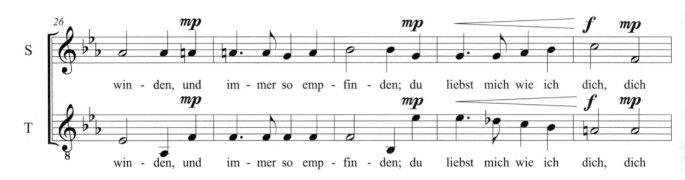

win - den, und   im - mer so emp - fin - den; du   liebst mich wie ich   dich,   dich

win - den, und   im - mer so emp - fin - den; du   liebst mich wie ich   dich,   dich

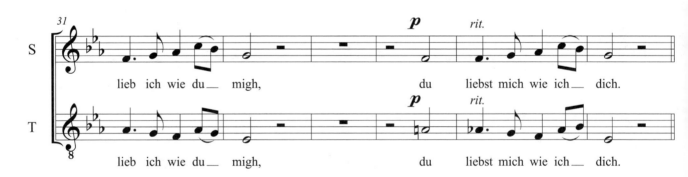

lieb ich wie du __ migh,   du   liebst mich wie ich __ dich.

lieb ich wie du __ migh,   du   liebst mich wie ich __ dich.

EX. 5.18 – Schütz, "Kleine geistliche Konzerte," mm. 1–18.

Schaf - fe in mir,   Gott, ein rei - nes Herz,

Schaf - fe in mir,   Gott, ein rei - nes

EX. 5.18 – continued

For the following excerpt, be sure to indicate the unisons and notes that are repeated consecutively between the voices.

EX. 5.19 – Skuhersky, "Benedictus," from *Missa a duas voces aequales*, mm. 1–15.

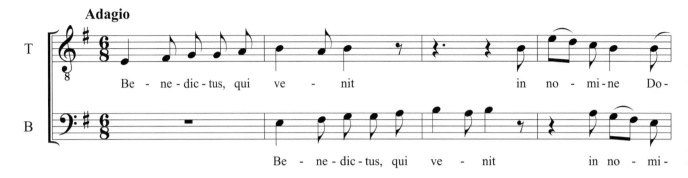

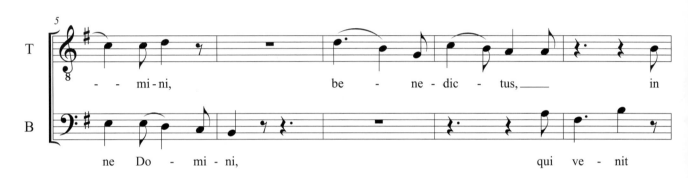

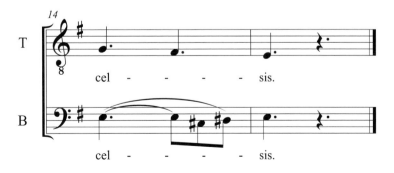

EX. 5.20 – Marcello, "To Thee, Oh Lord My God," mm. 1–11.

EX. 5.21 – Mozart, "Gloria," from *Missa Brevis*, KV 140, mm. 79–92.

EX. 5.22 – de Castro, "Ave Verum," mm. 1–15.

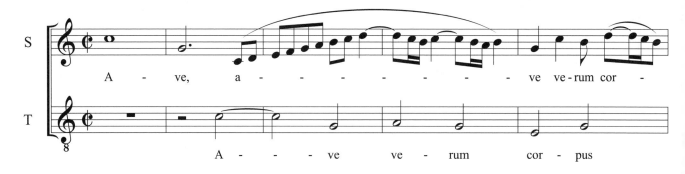

EX. 5.22 – continued

EX. 5.23 – Persichetti, "maggie and milly and molly and may," Op. 98, No. 3, mm. 3–22.

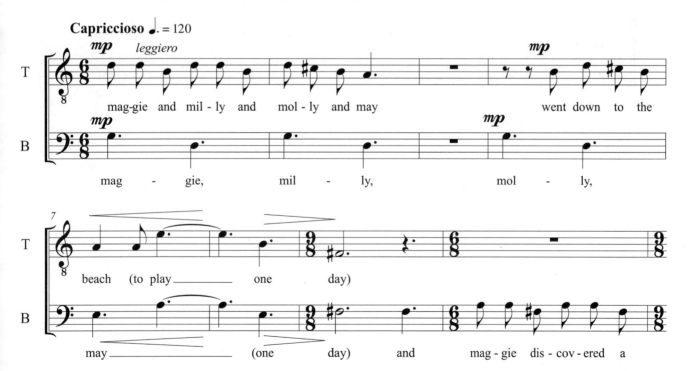

EX. 5.23 – continued

Chapter 6

Three Parts: Treble/Treble/Tenor

---

1 Introduction

Ensembles using two treble clefs and a transposing tenor are very rare, but studying the excerpts in this chapter will help familiarize you with reading tenor parts in a three-part texture. Whereas STB scorings are more common, the presence of a transposing part between two non-transposing parts (soprano and bass) may be a challenging introduction to three-part scores involving a tenor part. Before examining STB scores (see Chapter 7) it will be helpful to work on SAT scores where the left hand can play the transposing tenor part by itself while the upper voices are played by the right hand.

The biggest challenge with SAT scores is the visual incongruity created by seeing the lowest part (the tenor) occasionally higher than the upper two voices. Because the tenor always transposes down an octave (remember from Chapter 5?), it very rarely crosses either of the upper voices, but the visual overlap can still cause confusion. See **Ex. 6.1a** and **Ex. 6.1b** for a comparison. The first excerpt is written as SSA, while the second excerpt is identical insofar as it is performed, but looks significantly different written in an SST voicing.

Try playing through the first excerpt—it should look familiar from Chapter 4!

EX. 6.1a – Gounod, "Da Pacem," mm. 1–4, original SSA voicing.

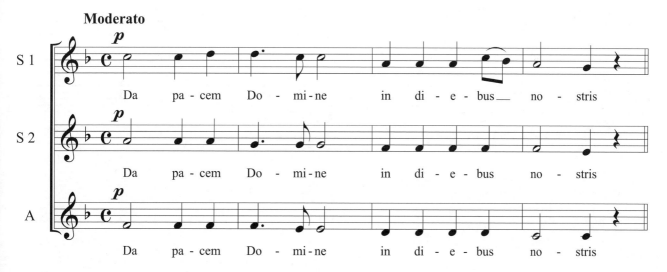

Now try playing through the next excerpt. Despite being the exact same musical material, the addition of the tenor part will require you to consider the transposition before beginning.

EX. 6.1b – Gounod, "Da Pacem," mm. 1–4, revised SST voicing.

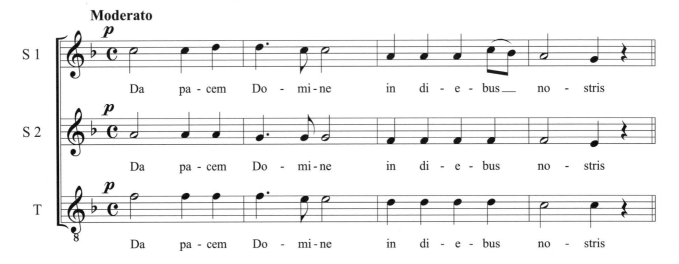

In order to maintain the tenor transposition in the midst of reading three parts, it can be helpful to identify periodic landmarks. In SAT or SST writing, the middle part will occasionally be at the unison with the tenor, or play the same note on consecutive beats. See **Ex. 6.2** for an example of this. Notice the line that has been drawn from the eighth note C in the third measure of the alto part to the quarter note C on the following beat in the tenor part. Despite the visual differences, this is the same C, and writing in a few of these indications can help you maintain the proper transposition.

EX. 6.2 – Traditional, "Auld Lang Syne," mm. 1–8.

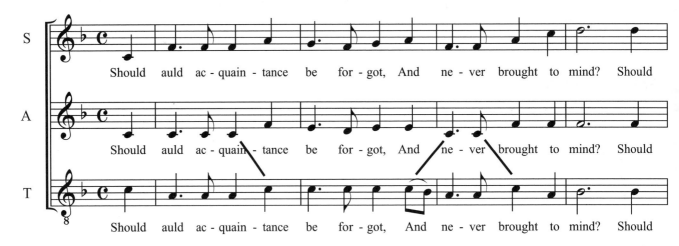

EX. 6.2 – continued

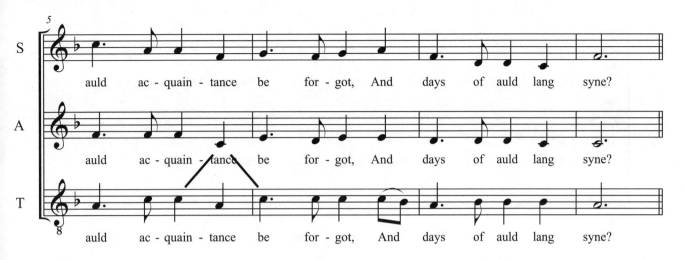

The following excerpt has a couple of similar situations—indicate these points in the score and use them to maintain your accuracy as you play through it.

EX. 6.3 – Bateson, "Your Shining Eyes," mm. 1–11.

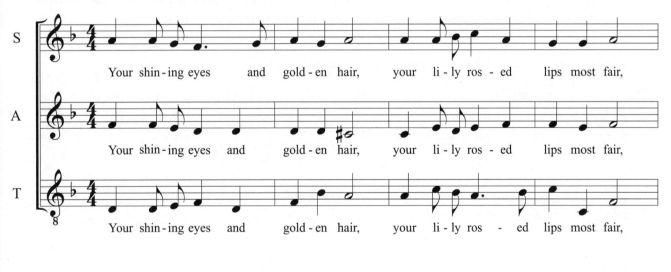

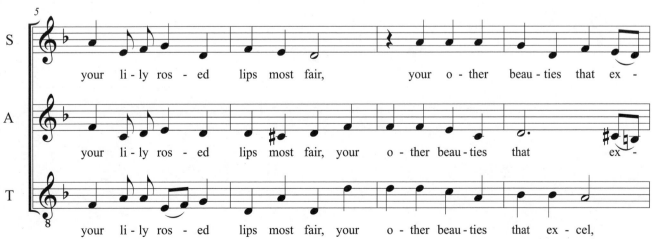

EX. 6.3 – continued

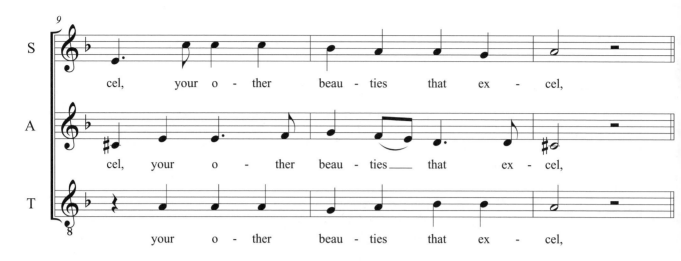

2 Sight-reading Exercises

In the following sight-reading exercises perform the soprano and alto parts with the right hand and the tenor with the left hand. Try to keep the tenor going! Because of the transposition, it can be difficult to come back in after dropping out for more than a note or two.

EX. 6.4 – Mendelssohn, "Nunc Dimittis," from *Three Motets*, mm. 49–53.

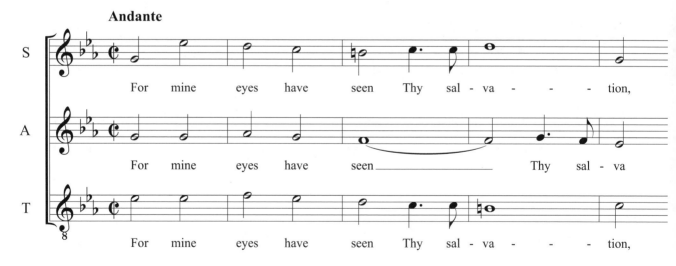

EX. 6.5 – Menegali, "Jesu, Salvator mundi," mm. 1–11.

EX. 6.6 – Turchaninov, "Voskresni," mm. 1–6.

Transliteration by Monique Oyallon

EX. 6.7 – Byrd, "Kyrie," from *Mass for Three Voices*, mm. 1–8.

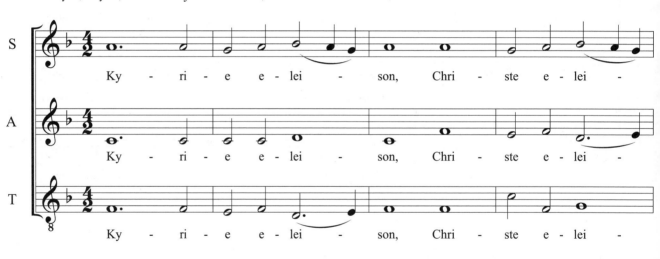

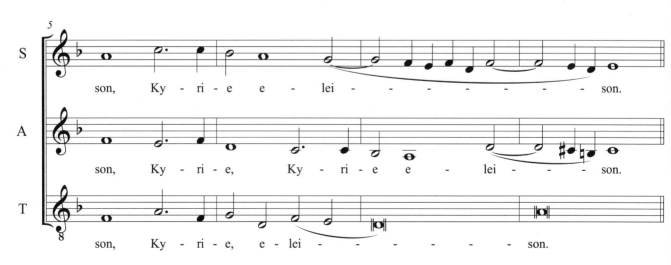

For the following excerpt, the tenor is significantly lower throughout.

EX. 6.8 – Gumpelzheimer, "Mit Fried und Freud fahr ich dahin," mm. 1–6.

EX. 6.9 – Byrd, "Credo," from *Mass for Three Voices*, mm. 91–96.

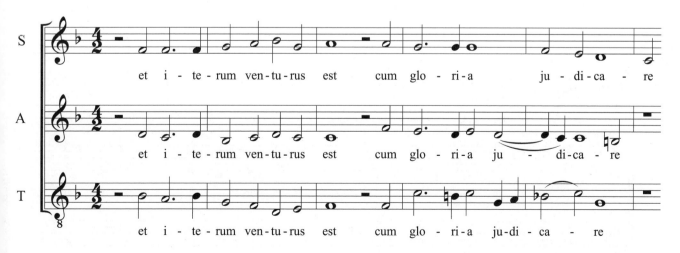

3 Prepared Exercises

The following exercises should be self-prepared. When preparing open score, feel free to mark your score with indications that will facilitate your performance of the work. Writing in fingering patterns, intervallic relationships and cautionary accidentals can help speed the preparation process.

EX. 6.10 – Weelkes, "Since Robin Hood," mm. 1–8.

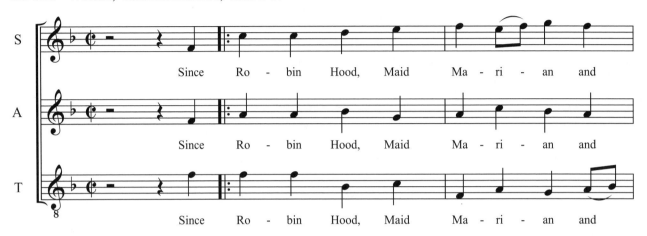

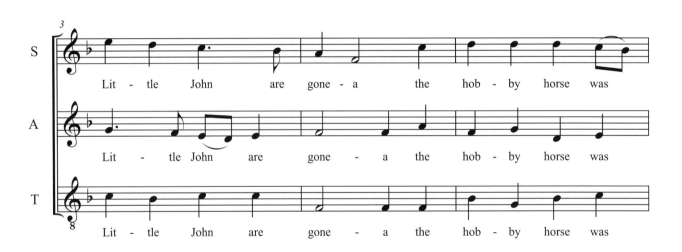

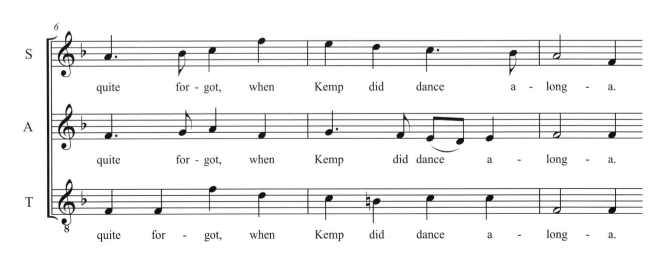

EX. 6.11 - Traditional French Carol, "Bring a Torch, Jeanette, Isabella," mm. 1–26.

EX. 6.11 – continued

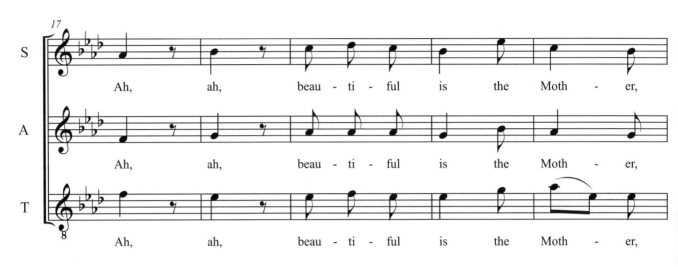

EX. 6.12 – Arr. Waller/Dwyer, "Shake the Papaya Down," mm. 37–44.

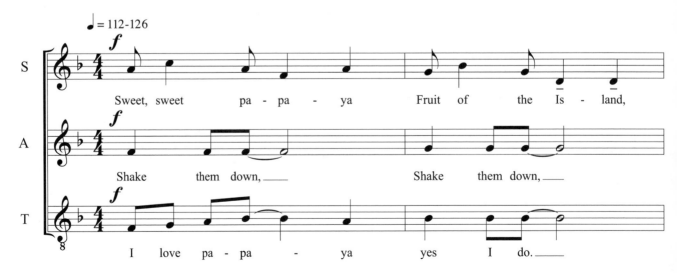

EX. 6.12 – continued

EX. 6.13 – Haydn, "An den Vetter," mm. 1–28.

EX. 6.13 – continued

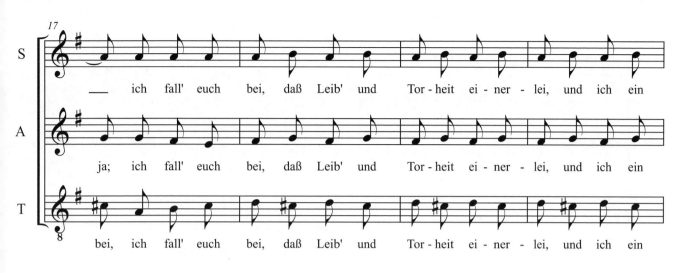

EX. 6.14 - Palestrina, "Jesu! Rex Admirabilis," mm. 1–13.

EX. 6.15 – Bach, arr. Canavati "Tears of Grief," from *St. Matthew Passion*, mm. 1–12.

Originally scored for SAB, presented here for SAT.

EX. 6.16 – Morley, "Though Philomela lost her love," mm. 11–20.

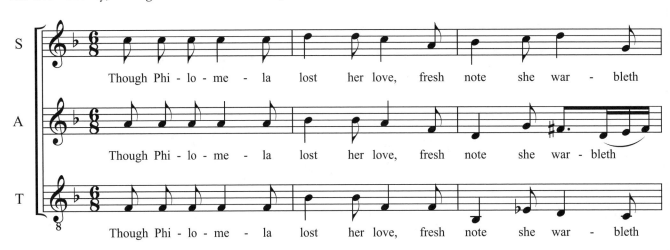

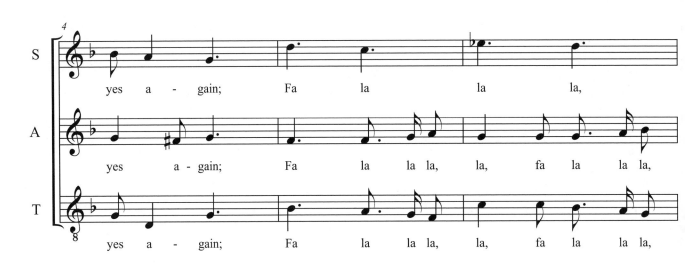

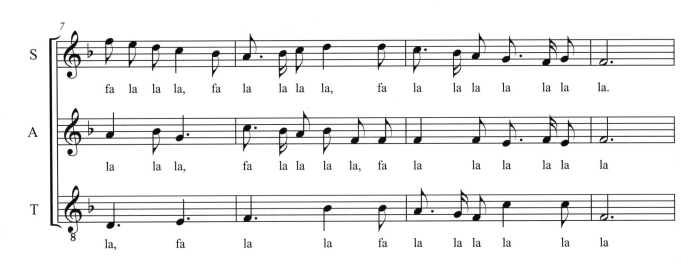

EX. 6.16 – continued

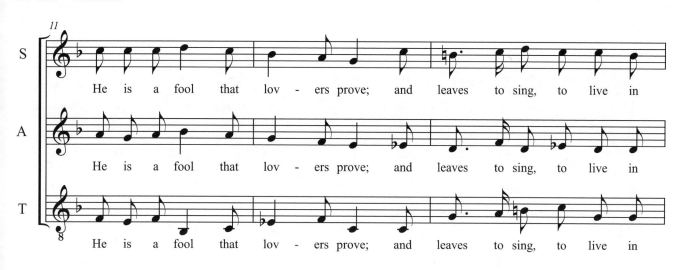

EX. 6.17 – Mozart, "Credo," from *Missa Brevis*, mm. 61–76.

EX. 6.18 – Byrd, "In Winter Cold – Whereat an Ant," mm. 1–14.

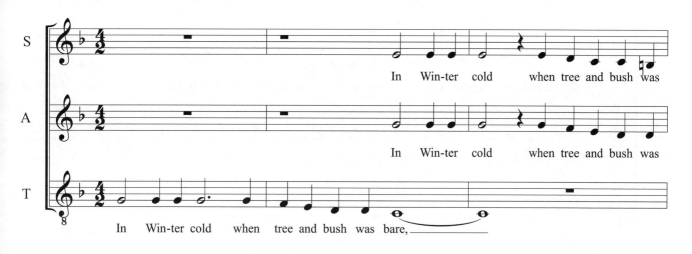

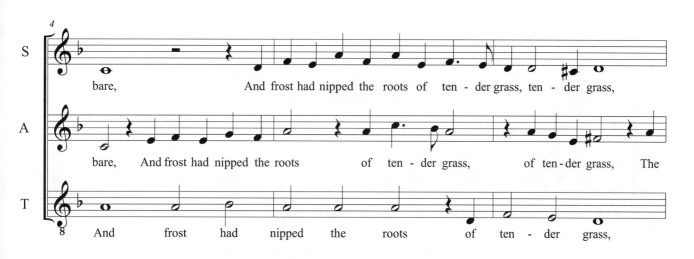

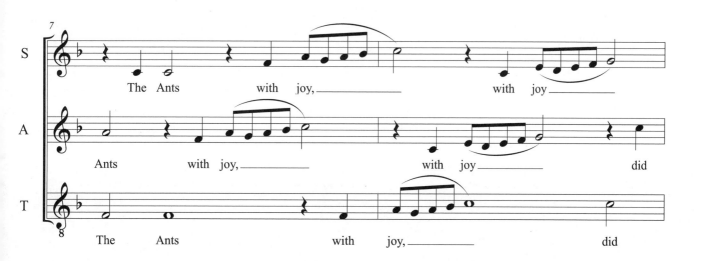

EX. 6.18 – continued

Three Parts: Treble/Treble/Tenor

In the next excerpt by Haydn (**Ex. 6.19**), look for a tricky two against three rhythm in the upper voices. The eighth note should come between the last two triplets of the grouping.

EX. 6.19 – Haydn, "An dem Veter," mm. 111–118.

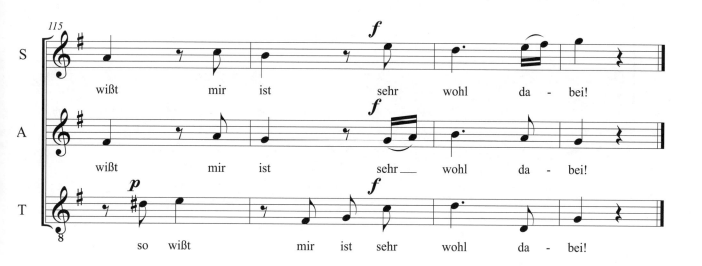

Look for occasional voice crossing in **Ex. 6.20**. Feel free to mark in where this occurs to help with your performance.

EX. 6.20 – Monteverdi, "Ave Maria," mm. 1–15.

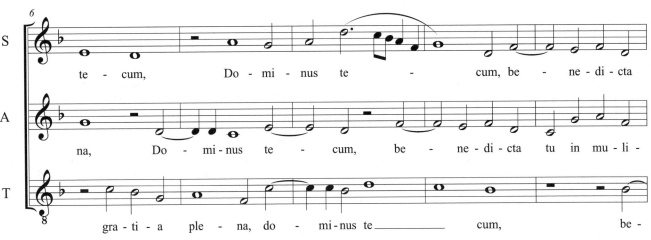

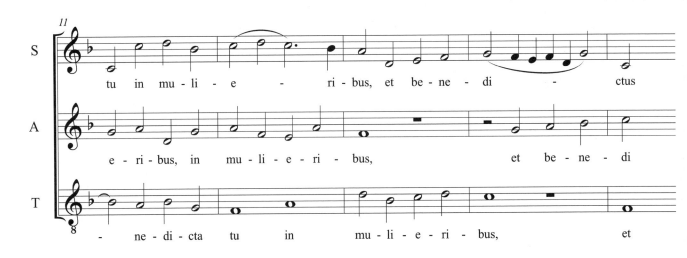

Chapter 7

Three Parts: Treble/Tenor/Bass

1 Introduction

Now that you are used to reading three parts including the tenor, learning to play the tenor in more challenging contexts is the next step. In Chapter 6 all three parts (SAT) used the treble clef with an octave transposition for the tenor part, but with the addition of a bass part, you must now sort out treble *and* bass clefs. An additional difficulty is that you will have to play the tenor and another part in the same hand. Previously you had played the women's parts (both of which shared the same clef) in your RH, and the transposing tenor part in the LH as shown in **Ex. 7.1**. Putting different clefs in the same hand will present a new challenge.

EX. 7.1 – Weelkes, "Since Robin Hood" (1608), mm. 1–4.

In many of the following exercises, you will have the opportunity to perform two parts in the *left* hand, as you see below in **Ex. 7.2**. As you prepare to play this excerpt at sight, identify the interval created by the tenor and bass parts when the bass enters.

EX. 7.2 – Clemens non Papa, Psalm CXL: *Domine clamavi ad te exaudi me,** mm. 1–4.

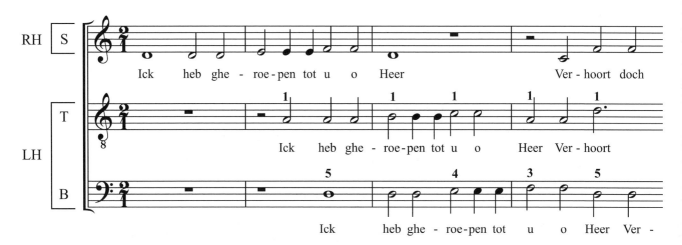

Note: The above excerpt comes from Clemens' Souterliedekens, *a collection of Psalms set to Dutch folksongs in the Dutch language. They are the oldest complete psalm rhyming in existence. The collection was published in 1557.*

You would normally encounter this type of open score in the following situations:

- A choral arrangement for women on one part (or a *divisi* part) and two men's parts
- A four part texture in which you want to focus on just three of the parts, including the tenor

While these situations are somewhat rare, playing STB scores is an important preparation for four part scores, in which you will frequently play both the tenor and bass parts in the LH.

As with the previous three part open scores, you should first analyze the score to decide which parts will be played with which hands. When compared with the previous chapters that focused on three part scores, you will find more examples where two parts will be performed by the left hand. The following discussion focusing on **Ex. 7.3**, William Caldwell, *Hail the blest morn!* will provide you with practice suggestions for performing two parts with the left hand.

EX. 7.3A – Caldwell, *Hail the Blest Morn!**, mm. 1–8.

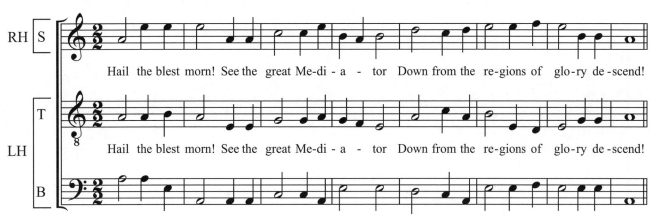

* ***Note:*** *When playing through this excerpt, you may notice the unusual voicings, especially those that create frequent parallel fifths and octaves. Caldwell wrote in the shape note tradition, otherwise known as the Sacred Harp tradition. This was a style of music for congregational singing popular in America in the nineteenth century, and is still used by some denominations, especially in the American South, today. Shape note music was most often scored for STB, omitting the alto part. Many contemporary editions include an alto part, added by an arranger or editor.*

Practice Techniques:

1. Start with tenor and bass in *two* hands – tenor in the RH and bass in the LH (**Ex. 7.3b**).
2. Play the tenor and bass in the *left hand alone* determining an appropriate fingering and writing this in the score (**Ex. 7.3b**).
3. Play through the right hand, again writing in your fingering.
4. Put all three parts together after you are comfortable with the above exercises (**Ex. 7.3c**).

Be careful, the two parts cross at one point! Circle the beat when this occurs before you start playing it at the keyboard.

EX. 7.3b – Caldwell, *Hail the Blest Morn!*, mm. 1–8, tenor and bass parts.

Do you remember where the tenor and bass cross? Be ready for it, especially after you add the soprano part!

EX. 7.3c – Caldwell, *Hail the Blest Morn!*, mm. 1–8, full score.

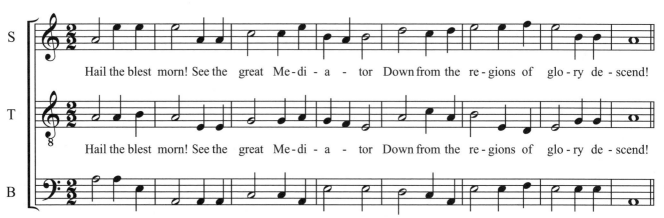

2 Sight-reading Exercises

In the following sight-reading exercises the soprano and tenor lines frequently demonstrate parallel motion, therefore it will be easiest to perform the soprano and tenor parts with the right hand and the bass line with the left hand. Try to keep the tenor going! Because of the transposition, it can be difficult to come back in after dropping out for more than a note or two.

Although there is no voice crossing in this excerpt, note where the soprano part repeats a note the tenors are holding (m. 7). You will need to play the tenor part's half note as a quarter note in order to play the soprano's D on beat two.

EX. 7.4 – Ravenscroft, *Of All the Birds that Ever I See*, mm. 1–8.

EX. 7.4 – continued

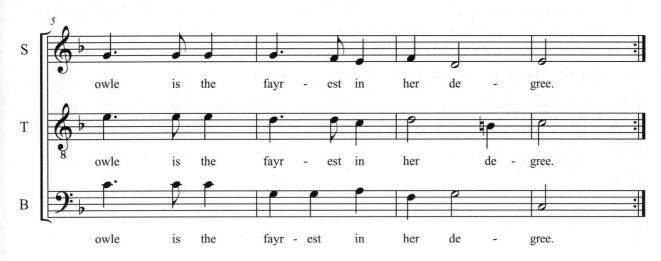

In the following two sight-reading excerpts the RH continues to perform the S and T parts.

The tenor part moves very little in this excerpt. Try keeping your right hand thumb on the D or C♯ in the tenor part throughout, allowing you to stay in one position and minimize the need to look at the keyboard.

EX. 7.5 – Traditional, "Angels We Have Heard on High," arr. for STB by Gregorich, mm. 1–4.

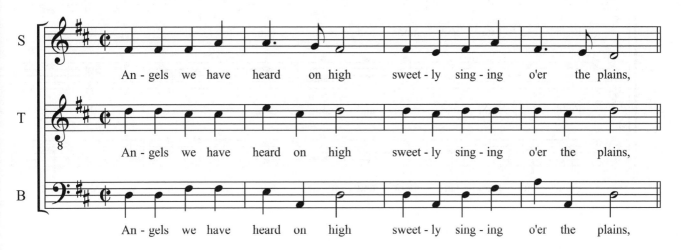

Circle the beats in which the soprano and tenor are *not* in thirds. Note that the bass part includes only the tonic and dominant throughout the first line. Use this information to minimize looking at the bass part, focusing your attention on the upper parts.

EX. 7.6 – Hopkins, Jr., "We Three Kings," arr. for STB by Gregorich, mm. 1–15.

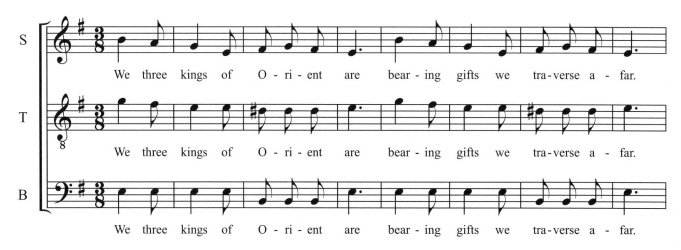

In the following example the tenor part could be played by either the RH or LH. Because of the parallel motion between the tenor and bass part, we recommend performing the tenor part with the LH.

EX. 7.7 – Haydn, *Betrachtung des Todes*, mm. 18–21.

3 Prepared Exercises

Prepare the following open score excerpts. Analyze the music to ascertain which parts will be played by the LH and which will be played by the RH. Writing in brackets or other reminders will be very helpful, as will indicating parallel motion between voices. As you prepare each excerpt, be sure to maintain a steady tempo.

EX. 7.8 – Cornysh, *Blow thy Horne Hunter*, mm. 1–12.

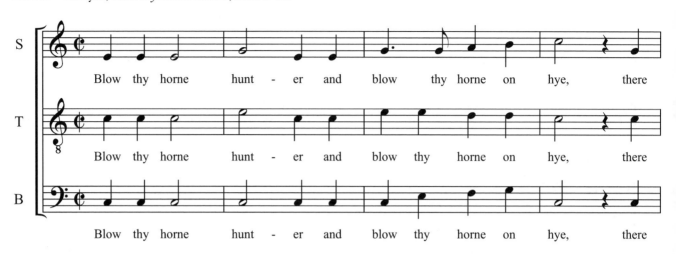

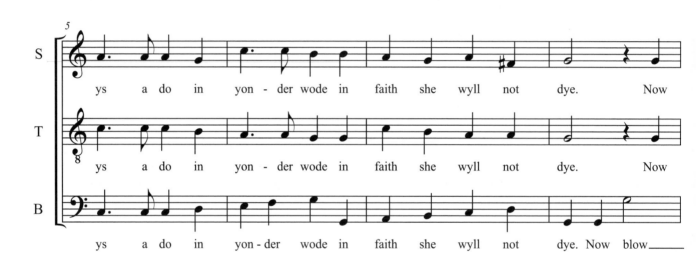

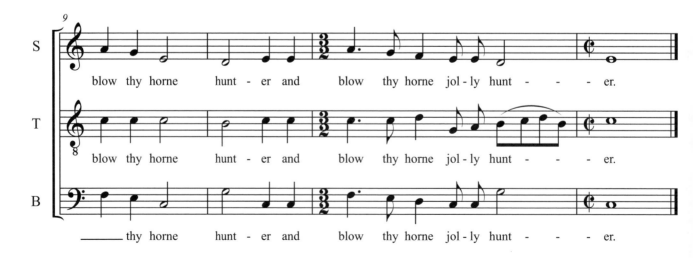

EX. 7.9 – Clemens non Papa, Psalm CXL: *Domine Clamavi ad te exaudi me* (1557), mm. 1–11.

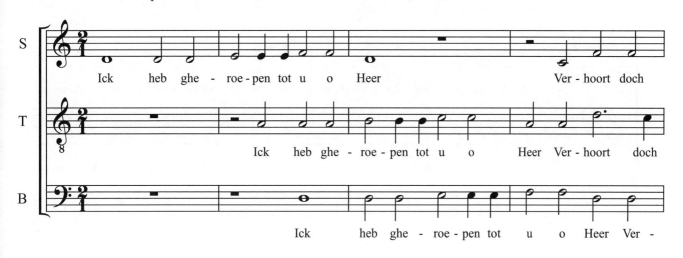

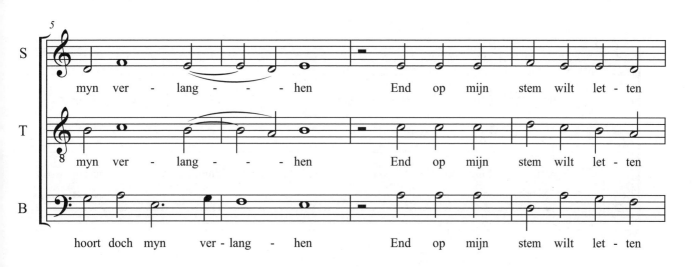

EX. 7.10 – Franck, *Domine non Secundum*, mm. 45–57.

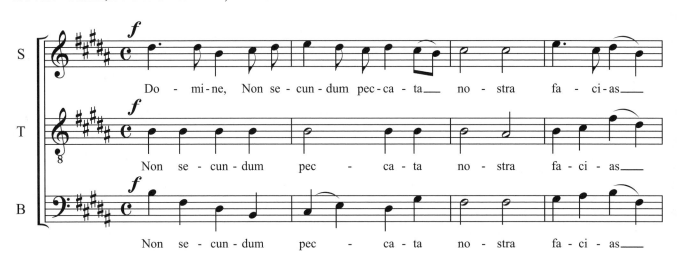

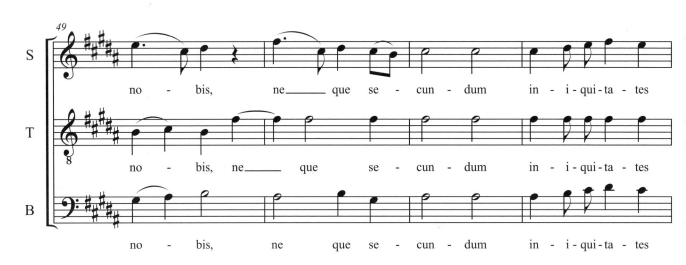

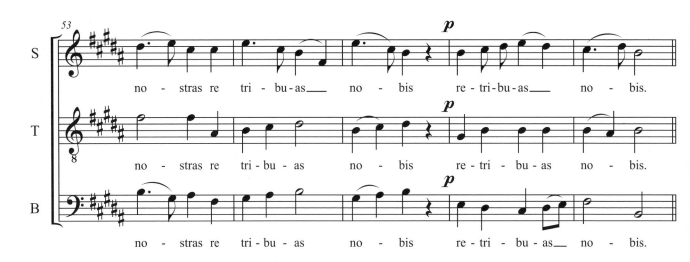

- This excerpt contains several voice grouping changes. It is very important that you write in where these are, and which voices will be grouped together at each point. The excerpt continues onto the next page.
- Note that in **Ex. 7.11** and in **Ex. 7.12** there are periods where the distances between the bass and tenor, *and* the tenor and soprano are greater than an octave. If your hand can comfortably reach a tenth, feel free to play this as written, but if you cannot reach that interval, you will need to choose a voice to omit. As has been discussed previously, the outer voices should be prioritized, but also be aware of the harmonic implications involved in your omissions. These excerpts will require extensive analysis and marking before keyboard preparation begins.

EX. 7.11 – Mozart, *Grazie agl'inganni tuoi*, KV 532, mm. 1–16.

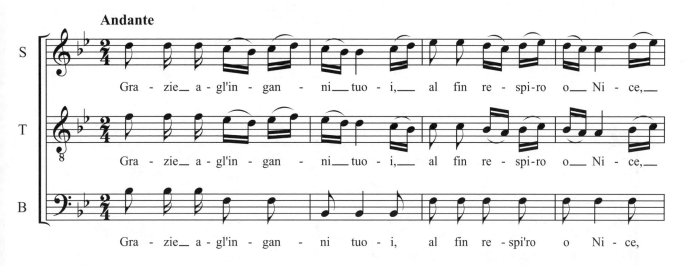

EX. 7.11 – continued

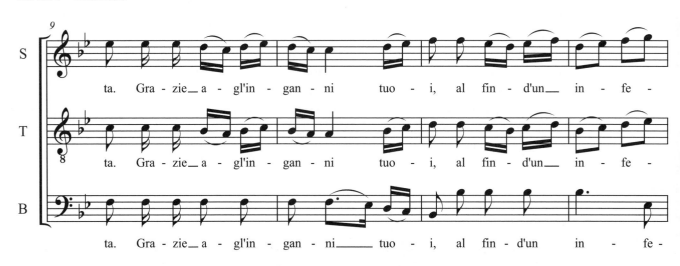

EX. 7.12 – Franck, *Offertoire*, mm. 57–79.

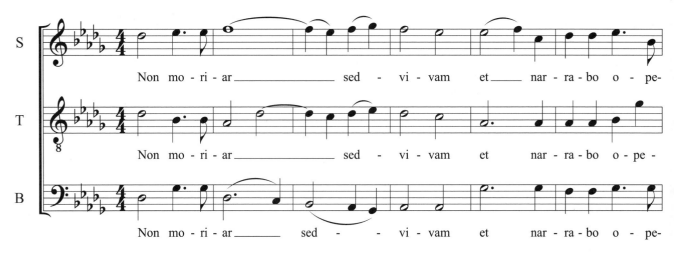

EX. 7.12 – continued

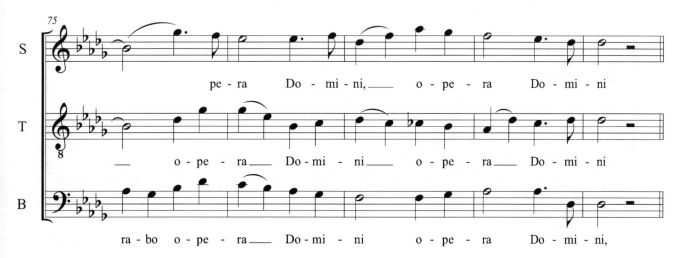

EX. 7.13 – Schubert, "Daß dereinst wir," from *Stabat Mater*, mm. 1–11.

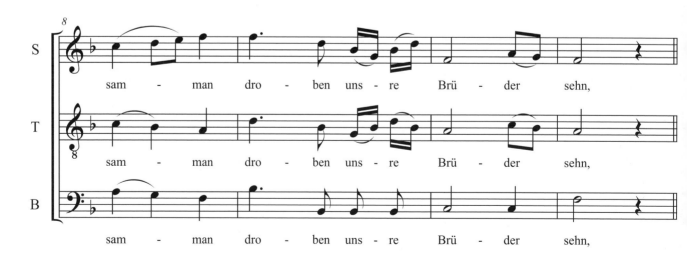

In ATB music, as you find below, it is more likely that you will encounter crossings between the top and middle voices. As always, make a note of voice crossings and voice groupings!

EX. 7.14 – Weelkes, "Cease Sorrow, Now," mm. 1–30.

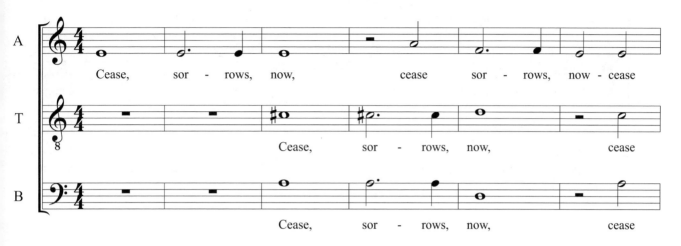

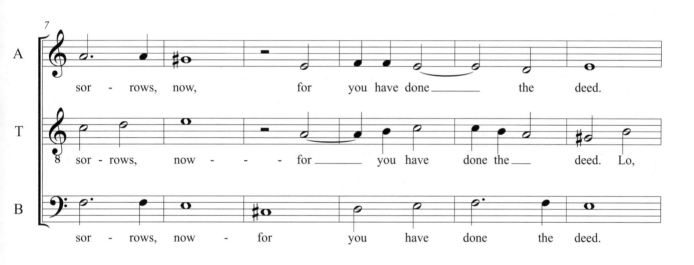

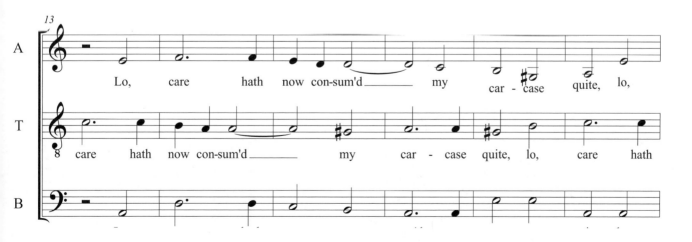

EX. 7.14 – continued

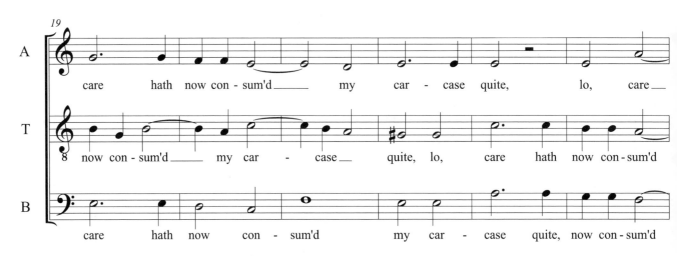

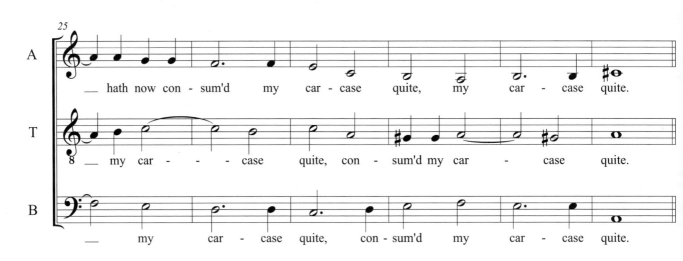

In the following SATB excerpt, perform just the STB parts. A SATB score has been presented here to allow you to practice reading selected parts from a full score. For additional practice try performing other three part combinations.

EX. 7.15 – Traditional English Carol, *The Boar's Head Carol*, refrain, mm. 9–16.

S: Ca - put ap - ri de - fe - ro Red - dens lau - des Do - mi - no,

A: Ca - put ap - ri de - fe - ro Red - dens lau - des Do - mi - no,

T: Ca - put ap - ri de - fe - ro Red - dens lau - des Do - mi - no,

B: Ca - put ap - ri de - fe - ro Red - dens lau - des Do - mi - no,

S: lau - des Do - mi - ni, lau - des Do - mi - no, Do - mi - no.

A: lau - des Do - mi - ni, lau - des Do - mi - no, Do - mi - no.

T: lau - des Do - mi - ni, lau - des Do - mi - no, Do - mi - no.

B: lau - des Do - mi - ni, lau - des Do - mi - no, Do - mi - no.

Chapter 8

Three Parts: Tenor/Bass Combinations

1 Introduction

For many pianists confronted with open choral scores, the most persistent technical challenge is reading the tenor part and making the octave transposition. The following excerpts are designed to present the tenor in a variety of contexts to improve your tenor reading. Note the *two* tenor parts in **Ex. 8.1**.

EX. 8.1 – Schubert, "Unendliche Freude," mm. 1–3.

In the next excerpt, note the dynamic markings. Including dynamics in your open score playing can help keep an ensemble engaged and listening. Conversely, omitting dynamics can set a bad example for your musicians!

EX. 8.2 – Schubert, "Die Zwei Tugendwege," mm. 1–8.

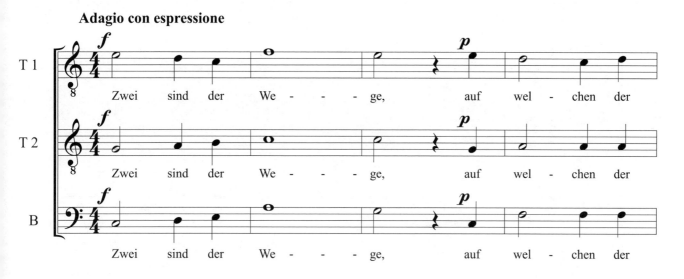

EX. 8.3 – Leavett, "Old Man Tucker," mm. 7–12.

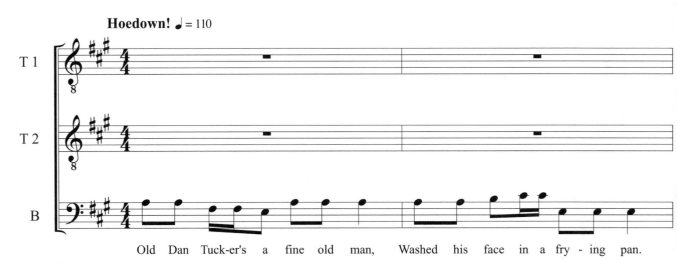

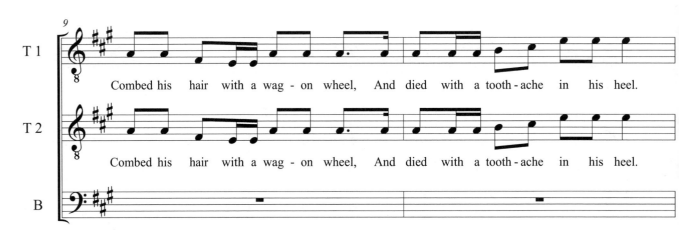

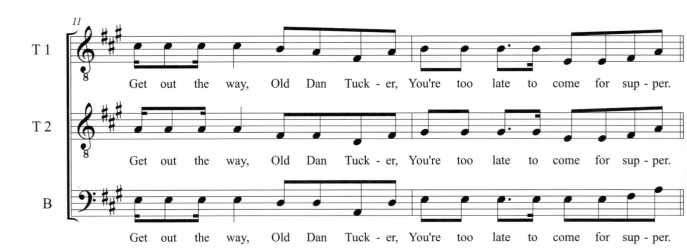

In the previous excerpt (**Ex. 8.3**), the bass enters by itself. Did you allow yourself to be surprised in measure 9 when the tenor entered? Or had you evaluated the score beforehand and placed your RH in the correct starting position?

Throughout this chapter you will find a combination of challenges discussed in earlier chapters, including voice crossing, wide leaps, and contrapuntal textures. Be sure to write in indications to help with your performances. In **Ex. 8.4** for example, look out for voice crossing in the upper two voices. They are both tenor parts, so they both transpose down an octave!

EX. 8.4 – Cornish, "Hoyda, Hoyda, Jolly Rutterkin," mm. 64–73.

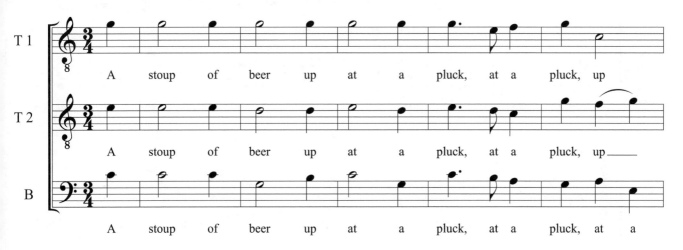

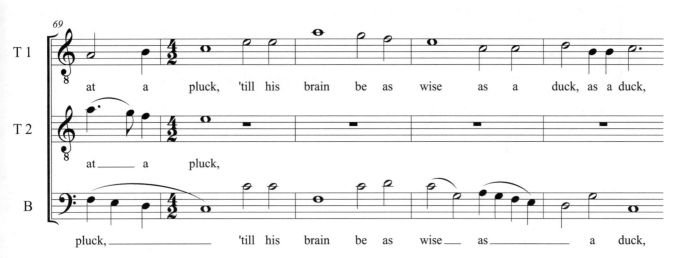

2 Sight-reading Exercises

EX. 8.5 – Traditional, arr. Gregorich, "Away in a Manger," mm. 1–17.

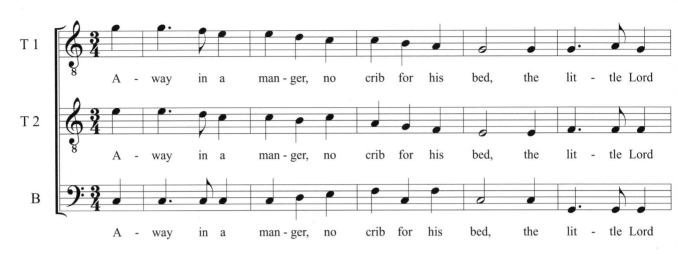

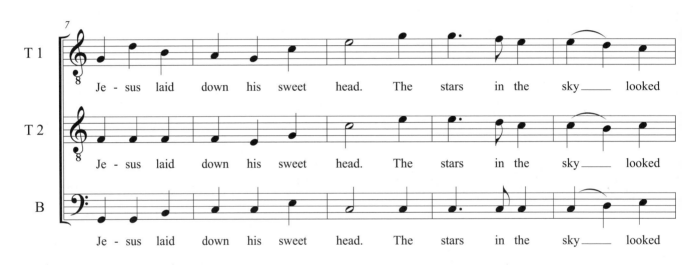

EX. 8.6 – Callcott,* "When Arthur First in Court Began to Wear Long-Hanging Sleeves," mm. 1–8.

* John Wall Callcott was a contemporary of Haydn and was known for composing "glees," of which "When Arthur First . . ." is one of his best known. Glees are short, a capella compositions, frequently based on popular poetry and frequently utilizing imitative writing, or "catches." Unlike most catches however, glees were intended for polite society and therefore avoided bawdiness and risqué material. Intended for gentlemen's clubs, they are often scored for two high parts (boy sopranos or tenors) and one bass part. Glee clubs soon became associated with colleges and universities, an association they retain today.

EX. 8.7 – Turchaninov, "Voskresni," mm. 7–10.

Transliteration by Monique Oyallon.

EX. 8.8 – Schutz, "Kleine geistliche Konzert," mm. 22–28.

EX. 8.9 – Traditional, arr. Shaw, "Joshua Fit the Battle of Jericho," mm. 10–17.

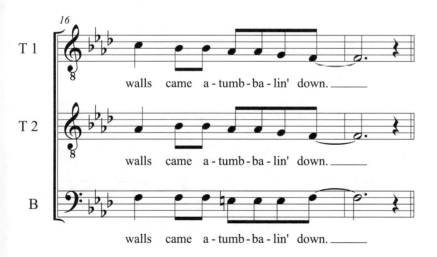

EX. 8.10 – Gounod, "Kyrie," from *Messe Breve*, mm. 9–16.

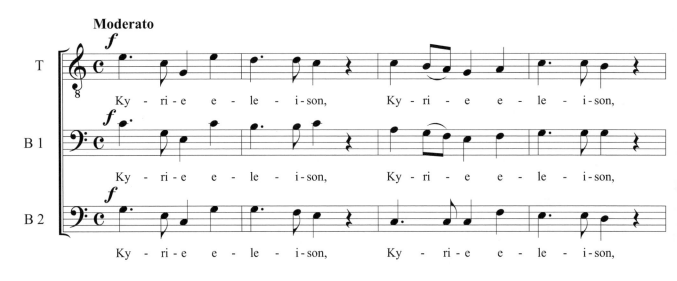

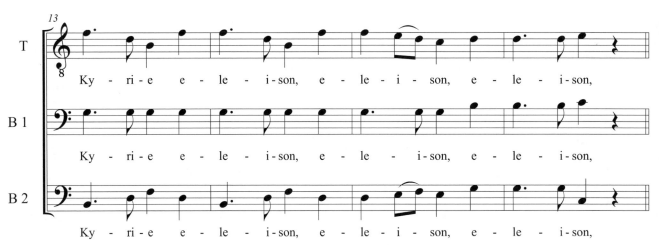

EX. 8.11 – Gounod, "Gloria," from *Messe Breve*, mm. 128–135.

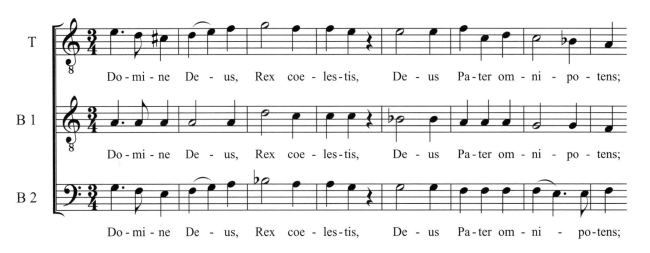

3 Prepared Exercises

EX. 8.12 – Weelkes, "The Gods Have Heard," mm. 1–20.

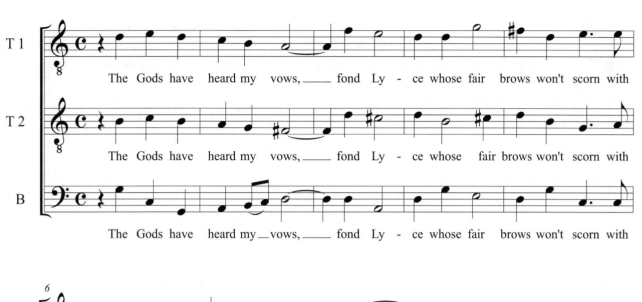

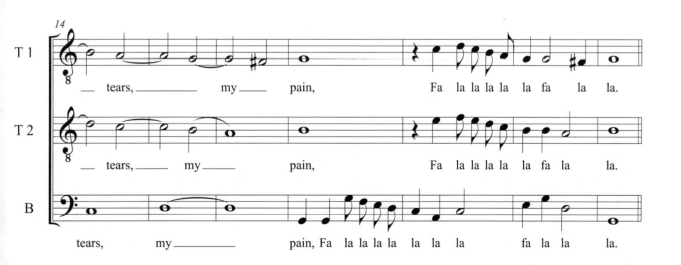

EX. 8.13 – Thompson, "The Pasture," from *Frostiana*, mm. 10–20.

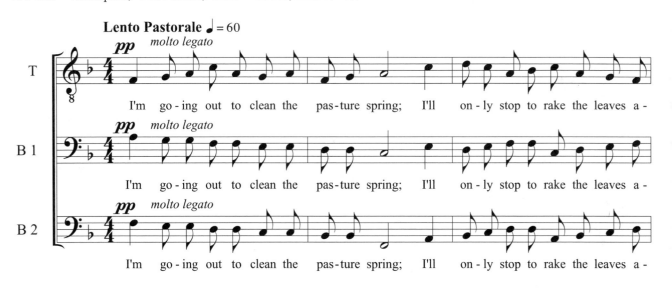

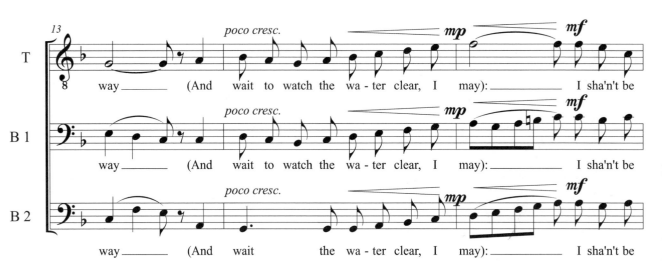

EX. 8.14 – Dubois, "Sanctus," from *Messe en Sol*," mm. 187–201.

EX. 8.15 – Dubois, "Kyrie," from *Messe en Sol*, mm. 6–21.

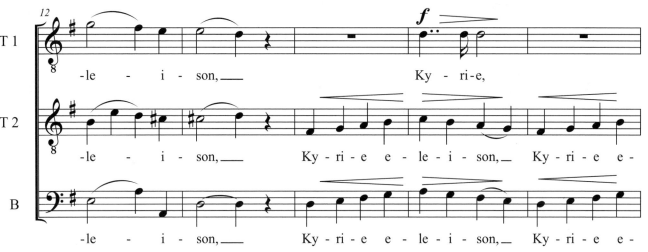

EX. 8.16 – Schubert, "Die Zwei Tugendwege," mm. 9–25.

T 1: Schließt sich der ei - ne dir zu, tut sich der and - re dir auf. Hand - delnd er -

T 2: Schließt sich der ei - ne dir zu, tut sich der and - re dir auf. Hand - delnd er -

B: Schließt sich der ei - ne dir zu, tut sich der and - re dir auf. Hand - delnd er -

T 1: ringt___ der___ Glück - li - che sie, Dul - dend der Lei - den - de.

T 2: ringt___ der___ Glück - li - che sie, Dul - dend der___ Lei - den - de.

B: ringt___ der___ Glück - li - che sie, Dul - dend der Lei - den - de.

T 1: Wohl ihm, wohl imh, den sein Ge - schick lie - bend auf bei - den ge - führt! ___

T 2: Wohl ihm, wohl imh, den sein Ge - schick lie - bend auf bei - den ge - führt! ___

B: Wohl ihm, wohl imh, den sein Ge - schick lie - bend auf bei - den ge - führt!

EX. 8.17 – Berlioz, "Chanson de Méphistophélès," mm. 72–81.

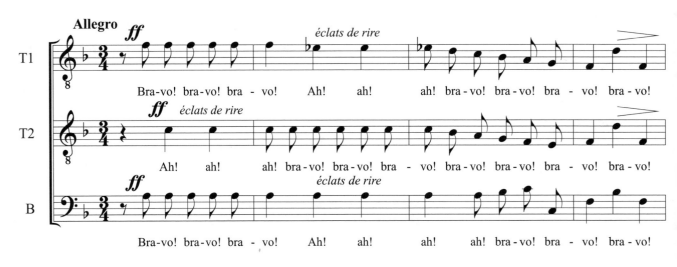

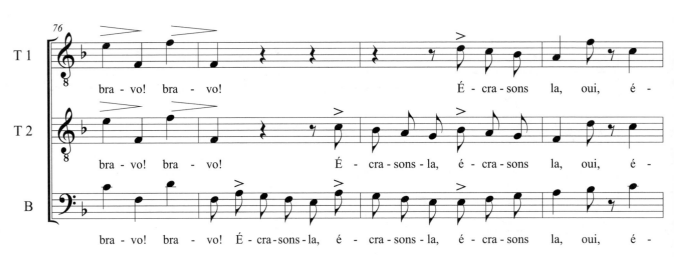

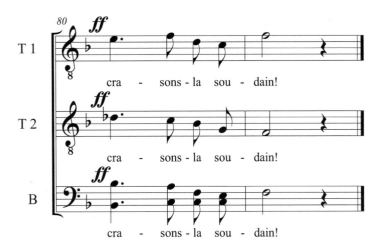

EX. 8.18 – Rorem, "The Corinthians," mm. 98–105.

EX. 8.19 – Schubert, "Majestät'sche Sonnenrosse," D. 67, mm. 1–28.

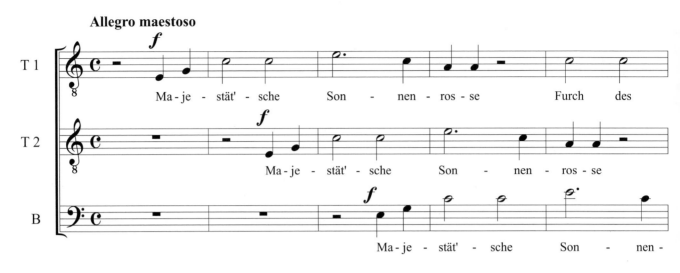

EX. 8.19 – continued

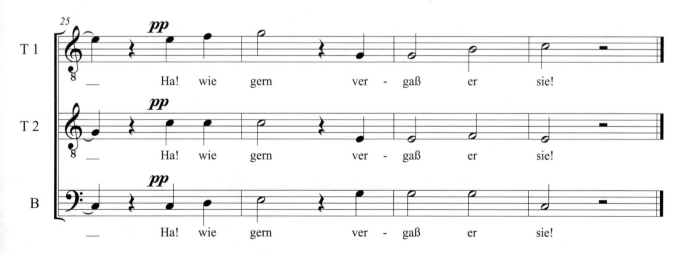

EX. 8.20 – Lotti, "Kyrie," from *Mass in B♭*, mm. 1–22.

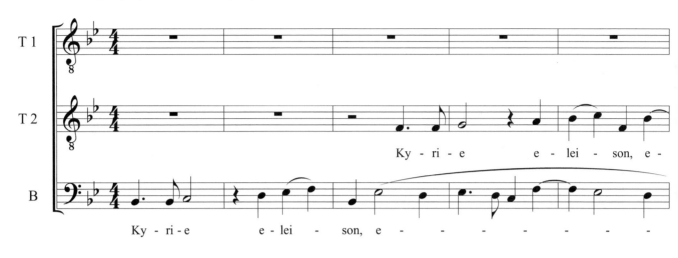

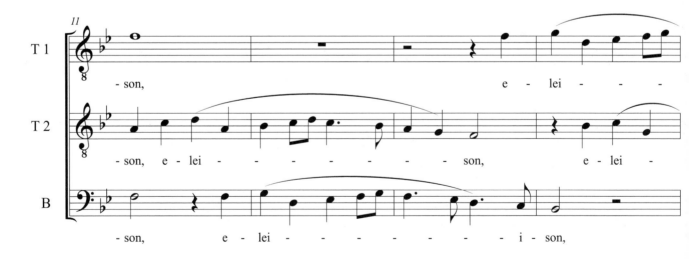

EX. 8.20 – continued

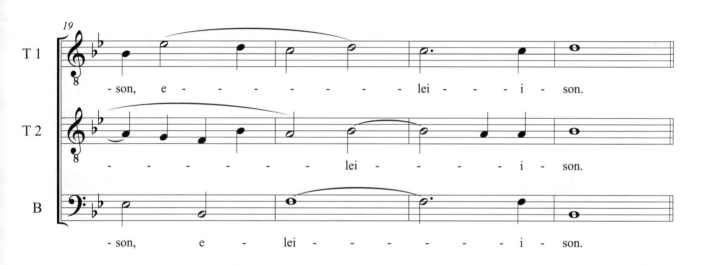

Part 3

Four Part Reading

Chapter 9

Four Parts: Soprano/Alto in RH, Tenor/Bass in LH

1 Introduction

You are now ready to move up to four part score reading. The addition of another staff may seem intimidating at first, but your training with three part scores should have equipped you with the skills necessary to perform two staves with one hand. While in previous chapters you applied that to just one hand, you will now transfer those skills to both hands simultaneously. In the vast majority of cases, you will either;

- split the parts evenly between the hands (SA in the right hand, TB in the left hand); **or**
- play the upper three parts (SAT) in the right hand and play the Bass in the left hand.

Although most open score reading requires you to switch between these groupings within a work, we will begin with exercises where the parts are evenly split between the hands. Instances of SAT/B groupings and excerpts where you will alternate between the two will be found in later chapters.

If it was important to look over a score before playing with two and three part scores, it is even *more* important to quickly examine a four part score before your first attempt at the keyboard. In many instances there may be passages with unisons, static pitches, or long phrases of parallel intervals between voices. Identifying the material you do *not* have to focus on is crucial when processing music spread over four or more staves.

In the case of unisons, for example, although a passage may be scored in four parts, it is effectively in only two or three. Look at **Ex 9.1** on the next page, and then play through it.

EX. 9.1 – Haydn, "Gloria" from *Paukenmesse,* mm. 1–8.

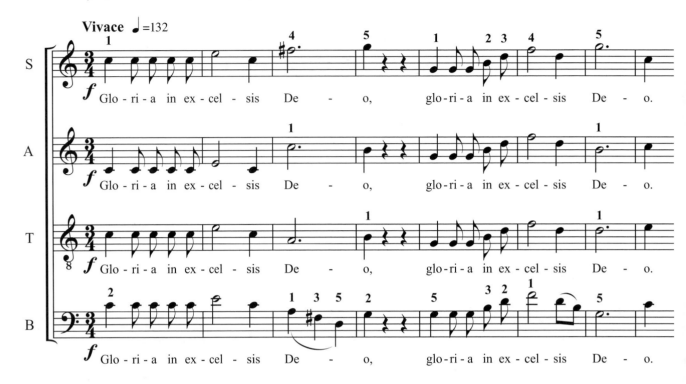

In the previous example, mm. 1–2 and 5–6 were effectively in two part texture – the soprano with one part, and the other three parts in unison an octave below. As always, writing in a few intervallic indications can aid in the performance of open scores, especially when dealing with four parts.

This example is in a true four part texture, but notice the static soprano line and the parallel thirds of the lower voices. Writing in these indications allows you to focus on just two main parts: the descending alto line and the ascending thirds in the tenor and bass.

EX. 9.2 – Haydn, "Agnus Dei" from *Paukenmesse*, mm. 13–18.

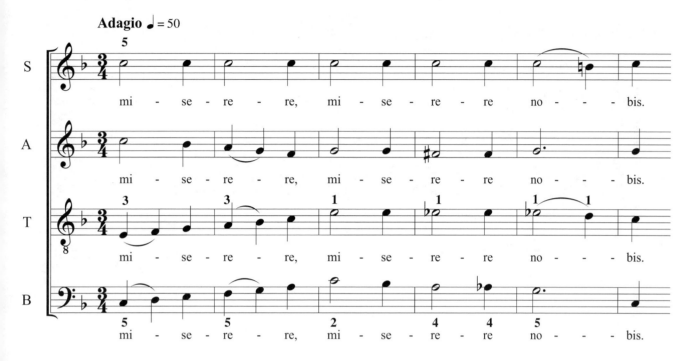

Identify the static lines and parallel intervals to reduce the amount of note reading you'll need to do.

EX. 9.3 – Schubert, *Hosanna Filio David*, mm. 1–8.

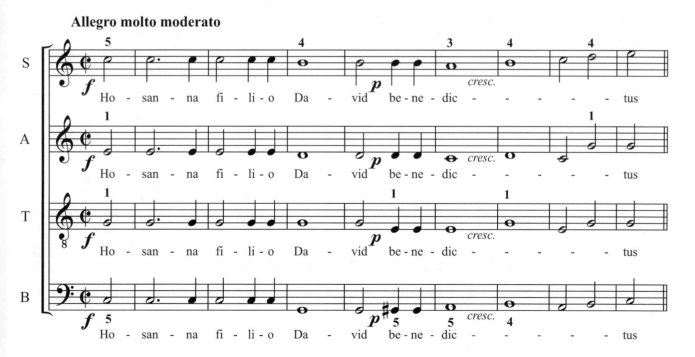

2 Sight-reading Exercises

For each exercise, quickly survey the score to identify static lines, parallel intervals, unisons and crossings. Using the open score shorthand you've developed, write in a few indications, then play through the exercise. Ex. 9.4 is more difficult than the two that follow it. It was placed first to eliminate page turns.

EX. 9.4 – Schumann, "Zigeunerleben," Op. 29, No. 3, mm. 3–10.

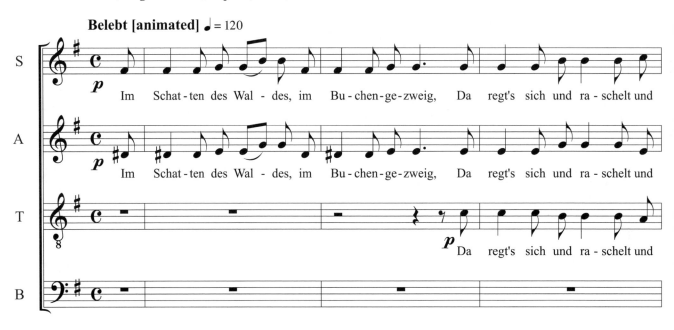

EX. 9.4 – continued

EX. 9.5 – Purcell, Chorus: "The Day that Such a Blessing Gave" from *Come ye sons of Art,* mm. 353–358.

* *Birthday Ode of Queen Mary, 30 April 1694. Originally for soprano, high counter-tenor, counter-tenor, and bass. Presented here for SATB.*

EX. 9.6 – Purcell, "Hush, No More," from *The Fairy Queen,* mm. 23–29.

EX. 9.7 – Haydn, "Et Resurrexit," from *Paukenmesse,* mm. 154–161.

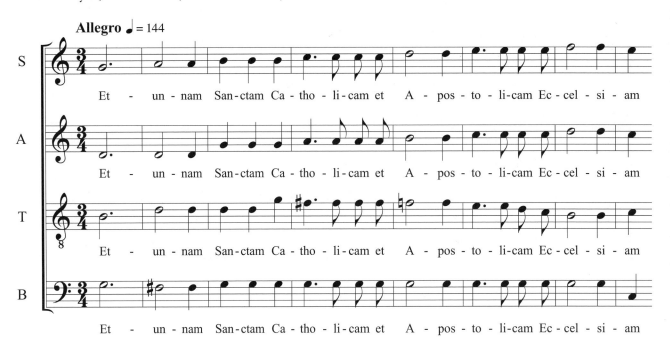

EX. 9.8 – Schramm, *For the Autumn Sky*, mm. 39–49.

EX. 9.9 – Liszt, *Ave Maris Stella*, mm. 5–12.

Try to observe the fingerings given in order to execute the phrasings in mm. 3–4.

EX. 9.10 – Mozart, "Ave Verum Corpus," KV 618, mm. 1–8.

Be sure to maintain rhythmic integrity with the dotted figures. Note that this figure is primarily parallel thirds—by focusing on the alto part and simply playing thirds above it you can avoid delays that could disrupt the rhythmic figure.

EX. 9.11 – Gruber/Reinecke, "Silent Night," arr. by Gregorich, mm. 1–12

EX. 9.11 – continued

3 Prepared Exercises

The following excerpts should be practiced over the course of several days or a week. While you might write in just a few indications for sight-reading excerpts, feel free to use more extensive indications for these, including fingerings, parallel intervals, and chords. As an additional exercise try performing some of the following excerpts as duets with a classmate—each person playing two of the four parts.

- In this first prepared exercise, identifying the static lines will give you the freedom to follow the moving parts.
- In mm. 8 and 10, take advantage of the repeated notes to look ahead to the next measure. Avoid the temptation to watch the repeated eighths and sixteenths instead of identifying the new intervals you move to in the subsequent measures.

EX. 9.12 – Schubert, "Kyrie" from *Mass in G*, D. 167, mm. 1–28.

EX. 9.12 – continued

EX. 9.13 – Davis, "The Birds' Noel," mm. 1–10.

EX. 9.13 – continued

Note that every measure except for m. 12 begins with repeated eighth notes. Utilize this repetition to look ahead and be ready for the shift on the second beat.

EX. 9.14 – Traditional Chanukah song, "Dreydl Song," arr. by Gregorich, mm. 11–16.

EX. 9.14 – continued

EX. 9.15 – Rameau, "O Nuit," mm. 1–21.

EX. 9.15 – continued

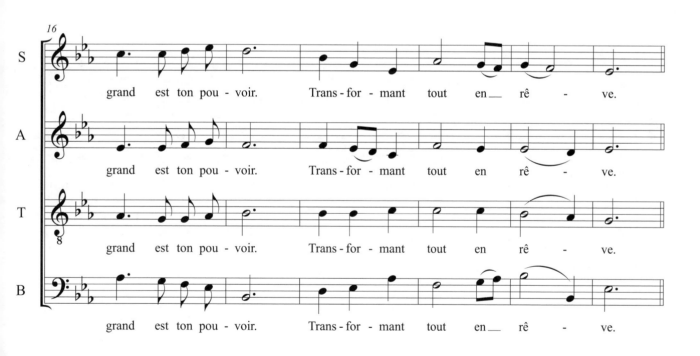

EX. 9.16 – Ravel, "Ronde," from *Trois Chansons*, mm. 12–25.

EX. 9.16 – continued

Although the atonal nature of this piece creates a considerable challenge, observing and indicating the frequent parallel thirds and sixths will make this difficult piece significantly easier.

EX. 9.17 – Webern, "Entflieht auf leichten Kähnen," mm. 1–9.

EX. 9.17 – continued

Chapter 10

Four Parts: Soprano/Alto/ Tenor in RH, Bass in LH

1 Introduction

The vast majority of four part scores can be grouped as SA–TB (upper voices in the right hand, lower voices in the left hand), SAT–B (upper three voices in the right hand, bass in the left hand) or a combination thereof. Having worked on SA–TB scores, it is now time to practice SAT–B scores.

Although it may seem unusual to group three parts in one hand, it is frequently the most convenient way to play an open score at the keyboard. The main reason for this comes from the wide spacing often found between tenor and bass parts. As you may recall from your study of music theory, voice leading rules call for no more than an octave between soprano and alto, and alto and tenor, but there is no restriction on spacing between tenor and bass. Even when spacing between the lower two voices is an octave or less, it rarely lasts longer than a few notes because of the disjunct nature of bass lines. See **Ex. 10.1**.

In situations like this, a pianist would need to reach a minor tenth to play this with a SA–TB grouping. For most pianists, it would be preferable to use an SAT–B spacing in order to play all the parts simultaneously. Try performing **Ex. 10.1** with both spacings to see for yourself.

EX. 10.1 – Brahms, "In stiller Nacht," mm. 1–2.

When performing open scores with SAT–B spacing, it is important to think of the upper voices harmonically. In many cases, the upper voices create a triad (or seventh chord) and learning to recognize these chords will make reading four part scores much easier. Here are some tips to quickly recognize if you have traditional, chordal harmonies in the upper voices.

- Look for spaces and lines. Because the upper voices all use the treble clef, the tell-tale thirds of a triad or seventh chord will frequently be all line notes or all space notes. Notice in **Ex. 10.1** that the diatonic triads in the pick-up measure and second half of measure 1 are all line notes for the upper voices. The same is true for all of the triads and seventh chords in **Ex. 10.2**, and **Ex. 10.3** as well.
- One accidental frequently means you have a secondary dominant chord. See the last two measures of **Ex. 10.2** below for an example. In this case, the F♯ indicates a D^7 chord, the applied dominant for the G minor chord on the fermata.
- Homorhythmic passages are frequently chordal. If the upper voices do not display rhythmic independence, it is often an indication of a chordal progression. Chorales are an excellent example of this. See **Ex. 10.3**.

Try performing this exercise and take full advantage of the half notes and whole notes to look ahead and identify the next harmony.

EX. 10.2 – Haydn, "Agnus Dei" from *Paukenmesse*, mm. 1–4.

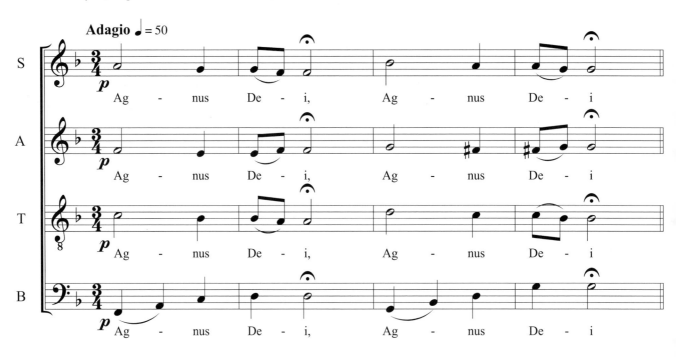

- For this example, and some of the others that follow, it is possible to perform portions with either SA–TB or SAT–B voice distribution. The purpose of this chapter is to develop abilities using SAT–B distribution, therefore we encourage you to use that distribution throughout this chapter.
- Chord names have been provided for the opening of this Psalm. Continue your analysis using lead sheet notation or roman numerals.

EX. 10.3 – Mason, Psalm 119: 153–160.

2 Sight-reading Exercises

- In this first sight-reading exercise, note that the upper voices are entirely comprised of diatonic triads.
- It may help to indicate the triad inversions for the upper parts. One suggested shorthand method has been indicated—feel free to develop your own shorthand.
- In order to focus on the RH, note that the LH part lies entirely in a five-finger position.

EX. 10.4 – Henry Purcell, "In These Delightful Pleasant Groves," mm. 8–11.

EX. 10.5 – Tallis, "If ye Love Me," mm. 1–5.

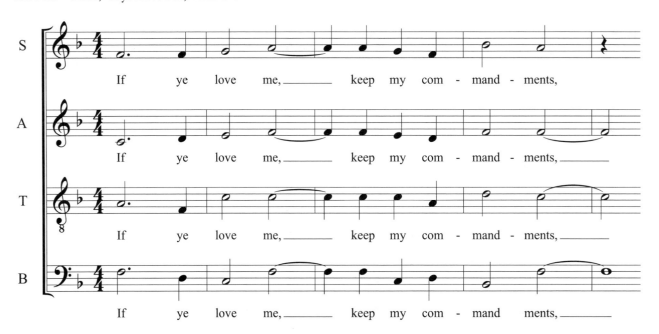

In this example, significant sections of the piece could be played in SA–TB groupings. Mm. 3 and 10–11 are the only instances where a SAT–B grouping is necessary. Nevertheless, we highly recommend using SAT–B grouping for the entirety of this selection to focus on the development of this skill.

EX. 10.6 – Schubert, "Zum Sanctus," from *Deutsche Messe*, D. 872, mm. 1–16.

For the following two sight-reading examples, take advantage of the repeated notes to look ahead. Despite the apparent activity in m. 2 of **Ex. 10.7** and m. 4 of **Ex. 10.8**, the pianist is advised to prepare for the following measures rather than read each of the repeated notes as it is played.

EX. 10.7 – César Franck, "Parole No. 1," from *Les Sept Paroles du Christ en Croix,* mm. 1–8.

EX. 10.8 – Schubert, "Sanctus," from *Antiphon for Palm Sunday,* mm. 1–6.

Note the voice crossing in m. 5 between soprano and alto. It may be helpful to indicate that beat 2 is simply a root-position I chord (A major triad), as is the final note.

EX. 10.9 – Dering, "Factum est Silentium," mm. 1–6.

The limited range of the bass in this excerpt lends itself to a convenient fingering (as indicated). This will allow you to focus on the three parts in the right hand.

EX. 10.10 – Farrant/Hilton, "Lord, for Thy Tender Mercy's Sake," mm. 1–5.

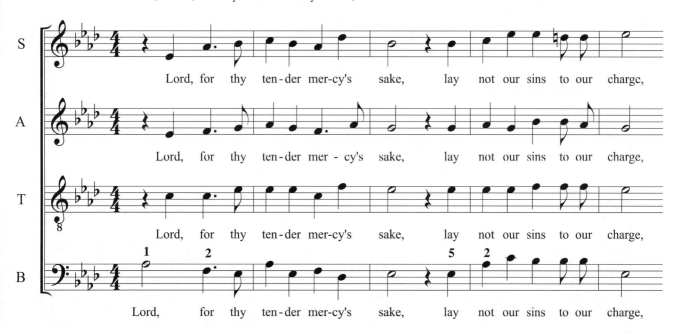

3 Prepared Exercises

As always, feel free to mark up the prepared exercises. For this chapter, it will be especially helpful to indicate chords in the upper voices and fingerings for the bass part.

EX. 10.11 – Tomkins, "I Heard a Voice," mm. 1–5.

In measure 16 there is a brief instance where the tenor part cannot be played with the RH. By omitting the tenor part and performing the cues that have been added, the excerpt can be performed in its entirety with the SAT parts in the RH.

EX. 10.12 – Schubert, "Credo," from Mass No. 1 in F Major, D. 106, mm. 7–27.

EX. 10.12 – continued

tem, fa-cto-em coe-li et ter - rae vi-si-bi-li-um

om - ni - um, et in - vi-si-bi - li - um.

In order to continue performing the SAT parts with the right hand throughout this exercise, in m. 44 you may use your right hand thumb to play *both* the alto A and the tenor G.

EX. 10.13 – Schumann, *Zigeunerleben*, Op. 29, No. 3, mm. 38–45*.

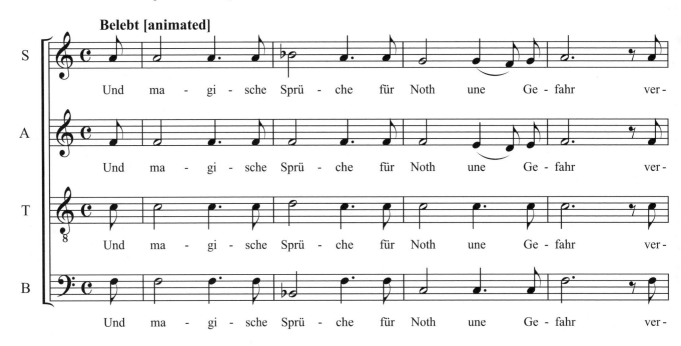

* The key signature for this work contains one sharp. Since this selection cadences in F Major, and then in C Major, the key signature has been omitted.

EX. 10.14 – Tchaikovsky, "Prositjelnaja Jektienja – Oche Nash," from *Goddelijke Liturgie*, Op. 41, mm. 35–42.

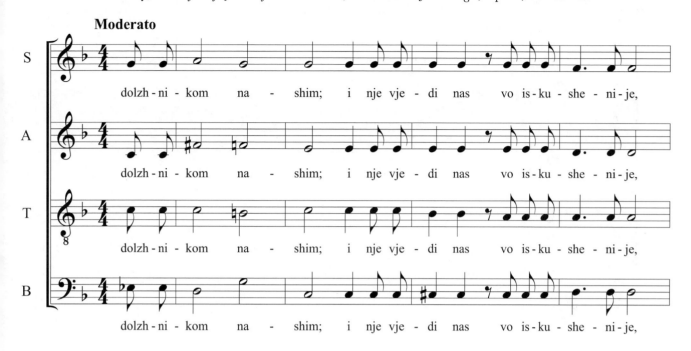

EX. 10.15 – Stanford, "The Blue Bird," Op. 119, No. 3, mm. 1–8, SATB excerpted.

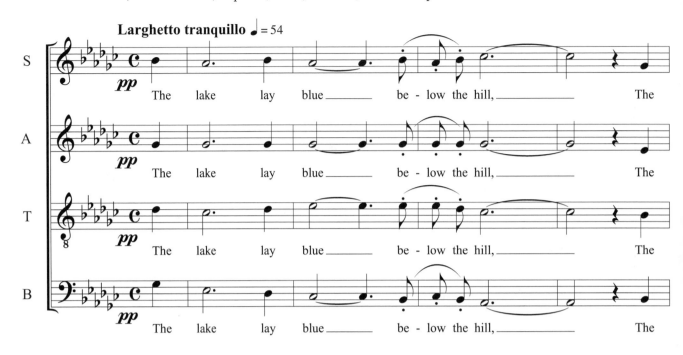

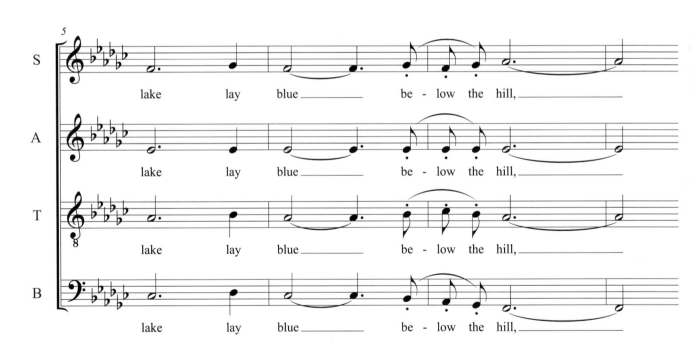

EX. 10.16 – Stanford, "The Blue Bird," Op. 119, No. 3, mm. 35–44, SATB excerpted.

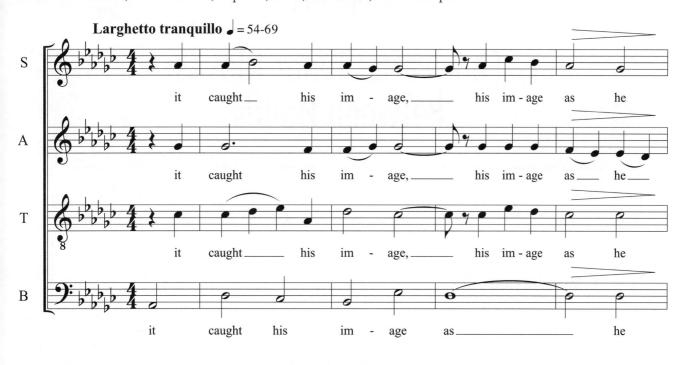

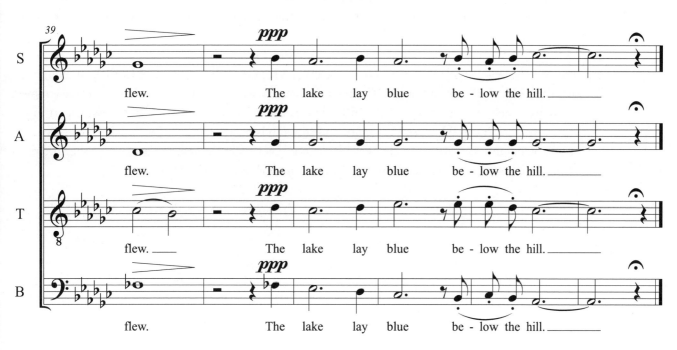

Chapter 11

Four Parts: Tenor Moves
Between Hands

---

1 Introduction

- Although it is easiest to maintain the same distribution of voices between the hands throughout the performance of an open score, in many instances this will not be possible. In most of these cases, it is the tenor part that will have to be moved between the hands. When you scan through an open score before playing, one of your first tasks is to examine the tenor part to identify where shifts between the hands will occur.
- In **Ex. 11.1** there are several points that necessitate shifting the tenor part from one hand to the other. The excerpt begins with the tenor a tenth below the soprano, which (in most cases) will require the pianist to play the tenor in the LH. On the third beat however, the tenor and bass parts have moved away from each other creating an eleventh. At this point you will need to play the tenor part in the RH, where the interval between the tenor and soprano is only a sixth.
- It will be helpful to mark these changes by writing brackets in the score to group together the parts to be played in the same hand. *Notice the brackets supplied for the following excerpt.*

EX. 11.1 – Mozart, "Heil, sei euch Geweihten!" from *Die Zauberflöte*, mm. 3–7.

The following comments refer to **Ex. 11.2**.

- Because it is most often the tenor part that necessitates changing the voice distribution between the hands, looking for large leaps in the tenor can help you identify these points. Notice the leap of a seventh from beat one to beat two in the first full measure below. This leap requires you to move the tenor part from the LH to the RH—write in a bracket to indicate these groupings.
- Also note the contrary motion between the tenor and soprano voices on the fourth beat of the same measure. Their expansion to the interval of a tenth requires you to move the tenor back to the LH. This could be done on the last eighth note of the measure, but it will be easier to make the switch on the second-to-last eighth note because the LH jumps up to a fifth below the tenor.
- Finally, keep in mind that it is more difficult to switch the voice distribution in the middle of faster notes (eighths, sixteenths), so if a voice shift is necessary, look for longer notes that will give you more time to change.

EX. 11.2 – Elgar, "Benedictus," mm. 13–15.

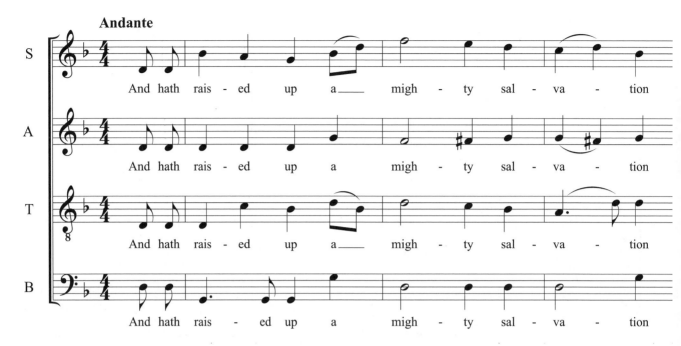

The following comments refer to **Ex. 11.3**.

- In the following excerpt, you must begin with the tenor in the RH, but on the downbeat of the second measure you have to switch the tenor to the LH because it creates an eleventh with the soprano. You could move back to a SAT–B distribution on the second beat, but notice that this distribution can only be maintained for a sixteenth note (or eighth note if you have bigger hands) before you need to resume an SA–TB distribution.
- It is usually preferable to maintain one distribution as long as you can, rather than rapidly switching the tenor between voices to maximize a preferred distribution. In this case, you can maintain the same distribution throughout each measure, switching only at the downbeat of the following measure.
- Again, write in brackets in **Ex. 11.3** to indicate where you will shift your voice distribution between SA–TB and SAT–B. Then play through the excerpt to evaluate the effectiveness of your choices.

EX. 11.3 – Elgar, "The Dance" from *Scenes from the Bavarian Highlands*, Op. 27a, mm. 29–36.

Finally, there may be instances where the tenor cannot be played by either hand, because its distance between both soprano *and* bass creates an interval larger than an octave. See the last note of **Ex. 11.4** for such an instance. The "C" in the tenor creates a tenth with the soprano and another tenth with the bass.

In such a situation, it is frequently best to roll the chord, carefully using the damper pedal to allow all four pitches to sound. In the example below, you could either roll the bass and tenor in the LH, or roll the upper three voices in the RH. Try both ways and see which you prefer.

EX. 11.4 – Gibbons, "Es sangen Gottes Engel," from *The Hymnes and Songs of the Church*, mm. 1–2.

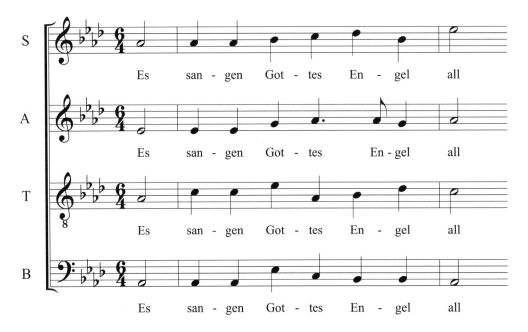

2 Sight-reading Exercises

For each sight-reading example, scan through the tenor to discover where you will need to redistribute the voices between the hands.

EX. 11.5 – Beethoven, "Credo," from *Mass in C*, Op. 86, mm. 360–369.

EX. 11.6 – Purcell, "The Mavis," mm. 1–11.

EX. 11.7 – Mozart, "Sanctus," from *Missa Brevis*, mm. 5–12.

Andante

EX. 11.8 – Pachelbel, "Magnificat," mm. 1–5.

EX. 11.9 – Mozart, "Abendruhe," mm. 1–20.

EX. 11.9 – continued

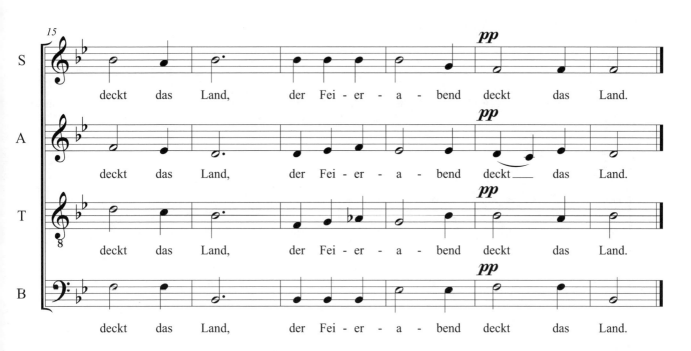

3 Prepared Exercises

For the following exercises, it will be helpful to identify where voice distributions shift by writing in brackets. It is also important to indicate where you may need to roll a chord because of large spacing between the tenor and the outer voices.

EX. 11.10 – M. Haydn, "Zur Kommunion," from *Deutschemesse*, mm. 1–6.

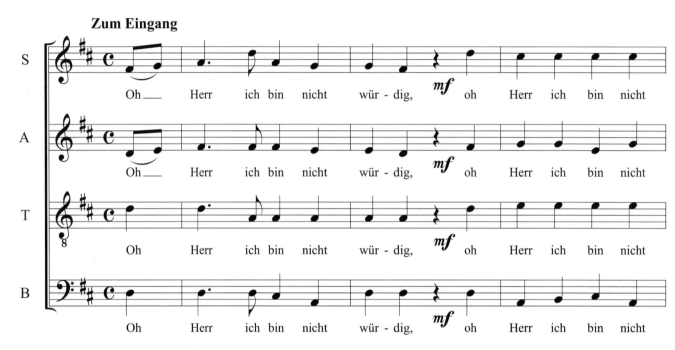

EX. 11.11 – Des Prez, "El Grillo," mm. 1–26.

EX. 11.11 – continued

EX. 11.12 – Gibbons, "Es sangen Gottes Engel," from *The Hymnes and Songs of the Church*, mm. 1–8.

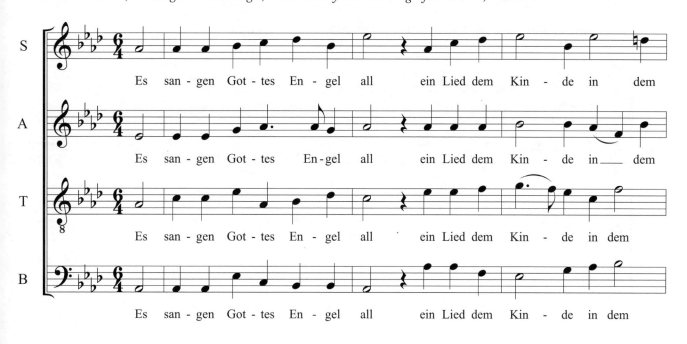

S: Es san-gen Got-tes En-gel all ein Lied dem Kin-de in dem

A: Es san-gen Got-tes En-gel all ein Lied dem Kin-de in___ dem

T: Es san-gen Got-tes En-gel all ein Lied dem Kin-de in dem

B: Es san-gen Got-tes En-gel all ein Lied dem Kin-de in dem

S: Stall, das für uns Men-schen kom-men ist, es ist der Her-re Je-sus Christ.

A: Stall, das für uns Men-schen kom-men ist, es ist___ der Her-re Je-sus Christ.

T: Stall, das für uns Men-schen kom-men___ ist, es ist der Her-re Je-sus Christ.

B: Stall, das für uns Men-schen kom-men ist, es ist der Her-re Je-sus Christ.

EX. 11.13 – Beethoven, "Kyrie," from Mass in C, Op. 86, mm. 1–11.

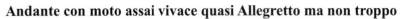

Andante con moto assai vivace quasi Allegretto ma non troppo

EX. 11.14 – Bortniansi, arr. Tchaikovsky, "Cherubim Song," mm. 1–24.

EX. 11.14 – continued

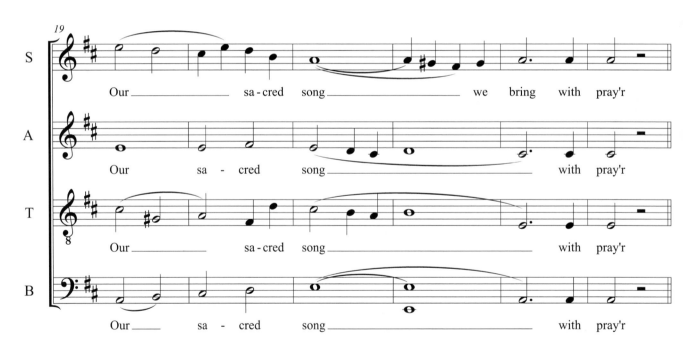

EX. 11.15 – Adler, "Hick's Farewell," from *Five American Folksongs*, mm. 9–14.

EX. 11.16 – Schubert, "Credo," from Mass in G, D. 167, mm. 1–20.

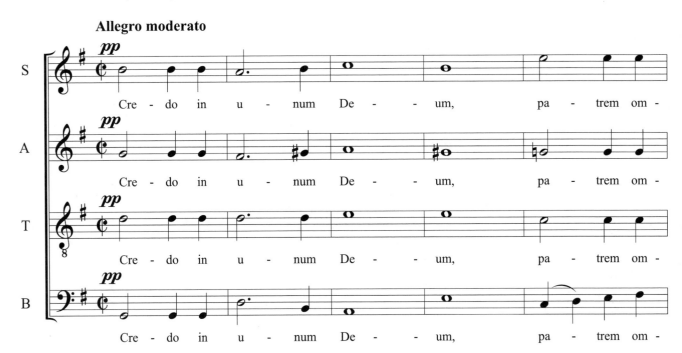

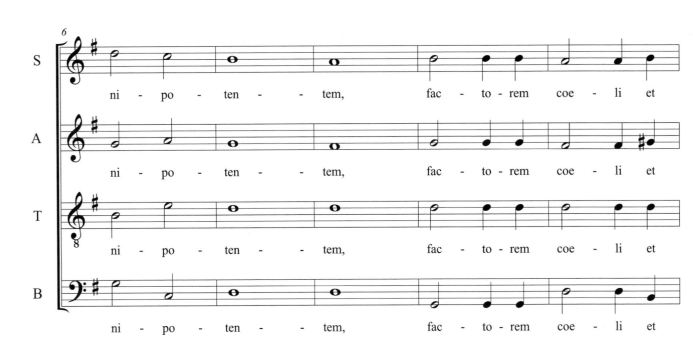

EX. 11.16 – continued

In this excerpt there are many places where triads can serve as landmarks as you perform the selection. Spend some time determining the location of these triads to assist you in learning this beautiful work.

EX. 11.17 – Barber, "Prayers of Kierkegaard," mm. 98–109.

EX. 11.17 – continued

Chapter 12

Four Parts: Highly Contrapuntal Textures

1 Introduction

You are now familiar with all of the most common four part voicings. Prior to this point, the majority of excerpts you have encountered have been largely homophonic, meaning that all four parts have the same or similar rhythms (see **Ex. 12.1**).

EX. 12.1 – Davis, "The Birds' Noel," mm. 1–4.

Dealing with contrapuntal textures in which two, three or even four separate rhythms are occurring simultaneously presents new challenges to the pianist (**Ex. 12.2**).

EX. 12.2 – Debussy, "Dieu! qu'il la fait bon regarder," from *Trois Chansons*, mm. 4–5.

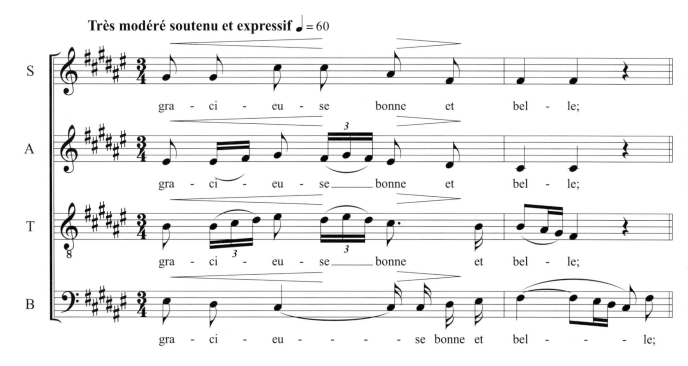

Try playing through these two excerpts and observe the increased level of difficulty in the contrapuntal Debussy song. When working on open scores containing contrapuntal sections, keep in mind the following suggestions.

- Identify where the contrapuntal sections occur and indicate this in the score. This can help you pace your practice time to focus on the more difficult passages.
- Continue to write in indications for parallel intervals, unisons, and voice crossing.
- Where imitation occurs, identify the melodic material that is imitated. Then be sure to bring out each entrance of the melody.
- Although it is always preferable to play all parts accurately, if you encounter difficulties in a performance it is important to maintain your effectiveness. This means keeping a steady tempo, clearly expressing the meter, and maintaining the outer voices.
- You should also practice playing various voice pairings, and individual parts at a performance tempo. You may also find it useful to play an individual part with one hand while conducting with the other hand.

Try applying these suggestions to **Ex. 12.3** below. Pay special attention to the entrances of the primary subject, labeling them for your convenience.

EX. 12.3 – Purcell, "The Day that such a Blessing Gave," from *Come, ye Sons of Art*, mm. 1–7.

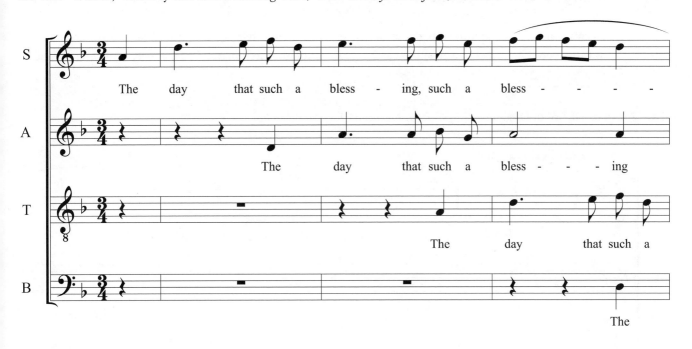

2 Sight-reading Exercises

Because most contrapuntal open scores are more difficult than their homophonic counterparts, the authors have included fewer sight-reading examples in this chapter, and more, lengthier prepared excerpts.

EX. 12.4 – Purcell, "With Drooping Wings," from *Dido and Aeneas*, mm. 1–7.

EX. 12.5 – Mozart, "Kyrie," from *Missa Brevis*, KV 49, mm. 1–5.

EX. 12.6 – Haydn, "Abendlied zu Gott," mm. 3–23.

EX. 12.6 – continued

EX. 12.7 – Elgar, "Great is the Lord," Op. 67, mm. 136–152.

EX. 12.7 – continued

3 Prepared Exercises

Many of the following exercises are lengthy. Imitative writing tends to create long phrases, and the authors chose to preserve musical integrity where possible, rather than truncate phrases in order to create shorter excerpts.

EX. 12.8 – Dvořák, "Come, Let Us Sing and Dance Together," from *Songs of Nature*, Op. 63 mm. 36–59.

EX. 12.8 – continued

EX. 12.9 – Dowland, "To Ask for All Thy Love," mm. 1–13.

EX. 12.9 – continued

EX. 12.10 – Sullivan, "Te Deum Laudamus," mm. 306–324.

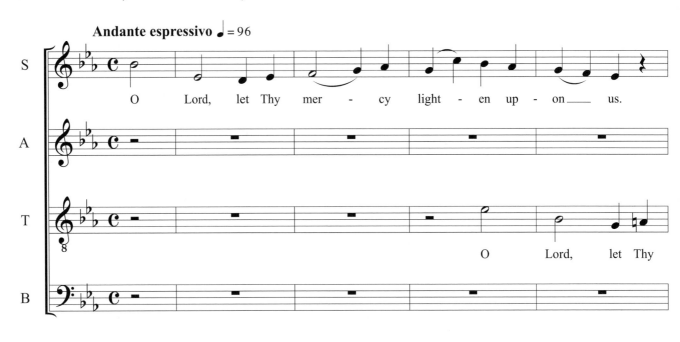

EX. 12.10 – continued

EX. 12.11 – Schubert, "Erben sollen sie am Throne," from *Stabat Mater*, D. 383, mm. 1–16.

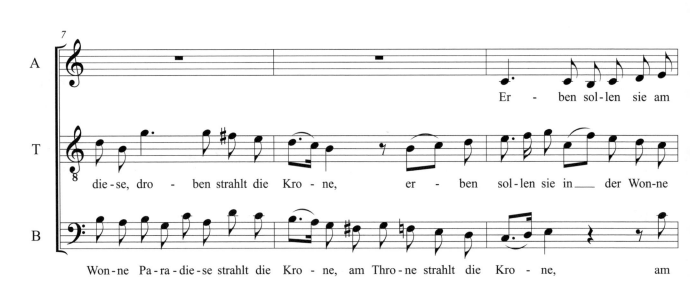

EX. 12.11 – continued

EX. 12.12 – Bach, "Christ lag in Todesbanden," BWV 4, mm. 1–8.

EX. 12.12 – continued

EX. 12.13 – Handel, "And the Glory of the Lord," from *Messiah*, mm. 11–38.

EX. 12.13 – continued

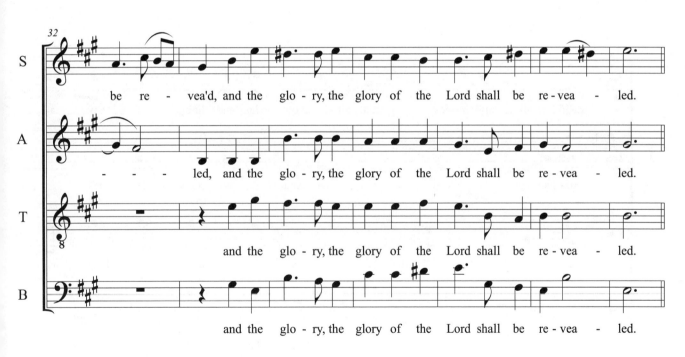

EX. 12.14 – Rorem, "The Corinthians," mm. 14–24.

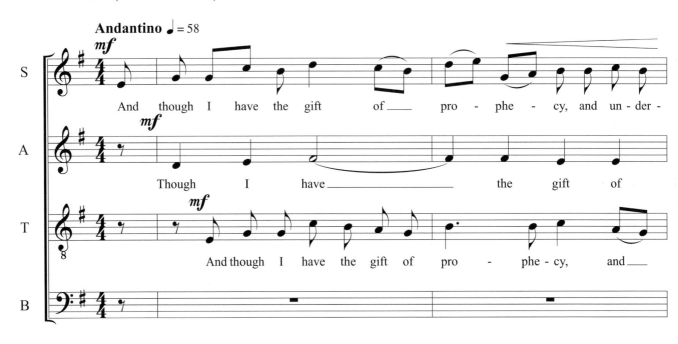

EX. 12.14 – continued

EX. 12.15 – Ravel, "Nicolette," mm. 27–39.

EX. 12.16 – Debussy, "Dieu! qu'il la fait bon regarder," from *Trois Chansons*, mm. 1–9.

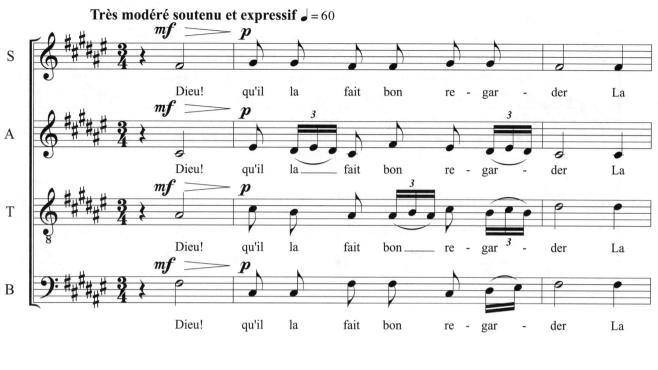

EX. 12.16 – continued

Part 4

Instrumental Part Reading

Chapter 13

Alto and Tenor Clefs

1 Introduction

Although you will rarely find alto and tenor clefs in choral music, they are used extensively in instrumental music. Alto clef is primarily used for viola parts, but can also be found in cello and trombone music, while the tenor clef is generally used for the upper range of the cello, double bass, bassoon, trombone, and bassoon. Both the alto clef and tenor clefs use the C clef. When positioned on the staff, the central point of the C clef defines middle C. For the alto clef, it is located on the middle line of the staff and for tenor clef, middle C is positioned on the second line from the top. **See Ex. 13.1.** For an easy reference point you may find it helpful to remember that the upper three lines of alto clef form a C Major triad, while the lower three lines form an F Major triad.

EX. 13.1 – Reference points for alto and tenor clefs.

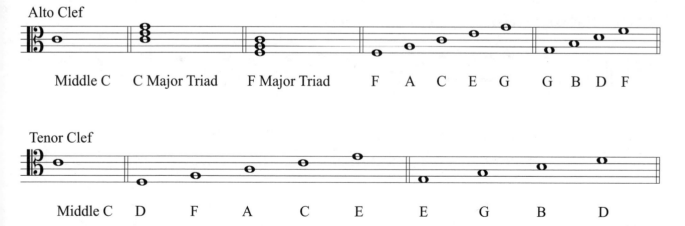

Learning to read a new clef requires practice, and the following exercises will provide you extensive opportunities to read from alto and tenor clef. The majority of excerpts include only two voices—one in alto or tenor clef and one in a different clef—but there are also examples of fuller scores from which you are asked to perform two or three selected parts.

To begin, read the following alto clef excerpt (**Ex. 13.2a**). You can check your accuracy by comparing it to **Ex. 13.2b**, the same excerpt translated to bass clef.

EX. 13.2a – Bach, Subject from "C minor Fugue," from *The Well-Tempered Clavier*, Book I. Alto clef example.

EX. 13.2b – Bach, Subject from "C minor Fugue," from *The Well-Tempered Clavier*, Book I. Notated in bass clef.

Now try similar exercises first notated in tenor clef (**Ex. 13.3a**) and then in bass clef (**Ex. 13.3b**).

EX. 13.3a – Traditional, "For He's a Jolly Good Fellow." Tenor clef example.

EX. 13.3b – Traditional, "For He's a Jolly Good Fellow." Notated in bass clef.

2 Sight-reading Alto Clef

EX. 13.4 – Traditional, "Row, Row, Row Your Boat," mm. 1–8.

EX. 13.5 – Beethoven, String Quartet, Op. 18, No. 2, movt. III, mm. 44–51. Violin I, viola, and cello excerpted.

In this example play the viola part with either the violin I or cello part.

EX. 13.6 – Beethoven, String Quartet, Op. 18, No. 2, movt. II, mm. 2–5. Violin I and viola excerpted.

EX. 13.7 – Haydn, String Quartet, Op. 20, No. 3, movt. I, mm. 1-7. Viola and cello excerpted.

EX. 13.8 – Mahler, Symphony No.1, movt. I, mm. 44–51. Viola and flute excerpted.

EX. 13.9 – Mendelssohn, Piano Trio in D minor, Op. 49, movt. II, mm. 9–12. Violin and cello excerpted.

3 Prepared Exercises Involving Alto Clef

In many of the following prepared exercises full scores have been provided. Prepare only the parts indicated.

EX. 13.10 – Finney, Piano Trio No. 2, movt. IV, mm. 90–106.

EX. 13.11 – Schumann, Piano Trio, Op. 80, movt. I, mm. 1–16. Prepare cello and violin only (omit piano).

EX. 13.12 – Beethoven, String Quartet Op. 18, No. 1, movt. III, mm. 1–16.

Prepare the viola part in combination with either the violin I or cello parts. For an added challenge prepare all four parts by performing the majority of the excerpt with the two violin and viola parts with the right hand and the cello part with the left hand. Occasionally portions of the viola part may need to be performed with the left hand.

EX. 13.13 – Haydn, String Quartet Op. 33, No. 1, movt IV, mm. 1–12.

Prepare violin I and viola. Look out for unisons between the two parts!

EX. 13.14 – Mozart, Symphony No. 40, movt. I, mm. 1–16. Violin I and viola excerpted.

Prepare violin and viola. Note that there are extensive voice crossings between the violin and viola parts so you may need to transpose the violin part up one octave.

EX. 13.15 – Bach, *Brandenburg Concerto* No. 3, movt. I, mm. 1–8.

EX. 13.16 – Schubert, *Trout Quintet*, Op. 114, movt. II, mm. 1–8.

Prepare viola and contrabass, which sounds an octave lower than notated. Then prepare viola and violin.

EX. 13.17 – Schubert, String Quartet, No. 14, movt. II, mm. 1–16.

EX. 13.17 – continued

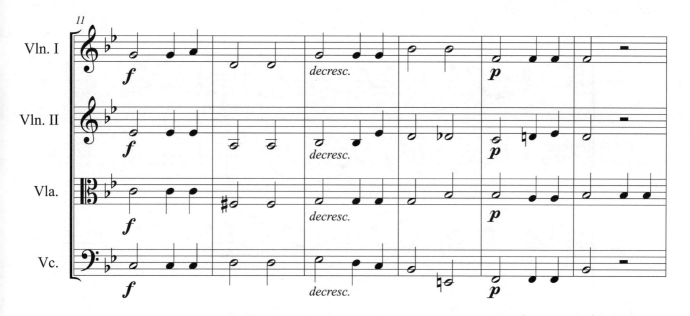

4 Sight-reading Tenor Clef

EX. 13.18a – Beethoven, Trio in B♭ Major for Piano, Clarinet, and Cello, Op. 11, movt. III, Var. VIII, mm. 1–4. Cello and piano left hand parts excerpted.

EX. 13.18b – Beethoven, Trio in B♭ Major for Piano, Clarinet, and Cello, Op. 11, movt. III, Var. VIII, mm. 9–13. Cello and piano left hand parts excerpted.

EX. 13.19 – Beethoven, Trio in B♭ Major for Piano, Clarinet, and Cello, Op. 11, movt. II, mm. 1–8. Cello and piano left hand parts excerpted.

EX. 13.20 – Borodin, *Polovtsian Dances*, mm. 72–79. Trombone I part excerpted.

5 Prepared Exercises Involving Tenor Clef

EX. 13.21 – Mendelssohn, Piano Trio in D minor, Op. 49, movt. II, mm. 9–12. Violin and cello excerpted.

*Note: You may remember this excerpt from earlier in the chapter (**Ex. 13.9**). In the earlier example the cello part was notated in treble clef; now it is presented in tenor clef.*

EX. 13.22 – Borodin, *Polovtsian Dances*, mm. 64–71. Cello and double bass parts excerpted.

EX. 13.22 – continued

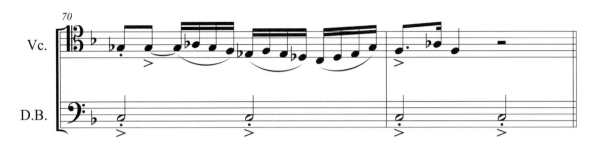

Please note that double bass parts sound an octave lower than notated. In the original notation the cello part uses bass clef beginning in m. 68. In this exercise tenor clef has been preserved throughout.

EX. 13.23 – Mozart, "Tuba Mirum," from *Requiem*, KV 626, mm. 1–18. Tenor trombone and bass solo excerpted.

EX. 13.23 – continued

thro - num,   co - get   om - nes   an - te   thro - - - - num.

EX. 13.24 – Beethoven, String Quartet, Op. 131, movt. II, mm. 108–120. Viola and cello parts excerpted.

Chapter 14

B♭ Transposing Instruments

1 Introduction

Reading transposing instruments at the keyboard can be a challenge, especially when you must play them simultaneously with a concert-pitched instrument, or instruments transposing to different keys. Unlike the alto clef, a transposing instrument uses standard clefs, but requires transposition by some interval other than an octave or unison.

The general principle with any transposing instrument is that when the performer reads a C on the staff, the sounding pitch is that instrument's transposition pitch. In the example below the stick figure musician is playing a B♭ clarinet. When he or she reads a C on the staff, the sound produced is a B♭, a pitch that corresponds to the clarinet's transposition. If the example below represented a person playing an E♭ horn, the pitch produced when playing a C would be an E♭. In some cases the sounding pitch may need to be adjusted up or down by an octave. These situations will be discussed as they come up in the following chapters.

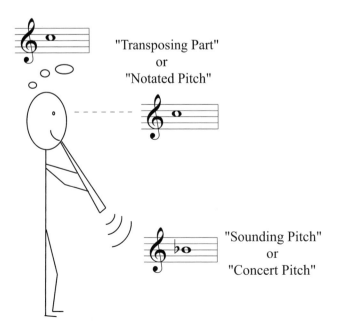

"Transposing Part"
or
"Notated Pitch"

"Sounding Pitch"
or
"Concert Pitch"

The interval of transposition for any B-flat instrument may be summarized in the following chart

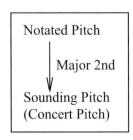

Notated Pitch

Major 2nd

Sounding Pitch
(Concert Pitch)

B♭ instruments are among the most common, and this chapter will provide you with exercises to allow you to become accustomed to these parts. You will frequently encounter B♭ transpositions when playing the following instrumental parts: trumpet, clarinet, soprano and tenor saxophone*, and occasionally trombone, tuba and euphonium. Begin by playing the following excerpt for B♭ clarinet (**Ex. 14.1a**). It should sound as **Ex. 14.1b**.

* *For a soprano and tenor saxophone example, please see **Ex. 15.12** on p. 288.*

EX. 14.1a – "Yankee Doodle," scored for B♭ clarinet.

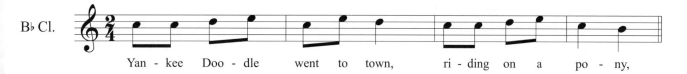

EX. 14.1b – "Yankee Doodle," scored for piano or other concert-pitched instrument.

Because B♭ is only a whole step below C, it can be helpful to think of moving every note down a step. If you are skilled at reading tenor clef you may use this ability to assist with transposing a melody down a major second. Compare **Ex. 14.1a** with **Ex. 14.1c**. Notice that the notes align on the same set of lines and spaces on the staff. **Ex. 14.1c** would sound an octave lower than **Ex. 14.1a**, so if you use this technique you will need to make the appropriate octave adjustment in addition to providing the key signature for the transposed key. This new key will always involve the addition of two flats or the removal of two sharps, or the combination of the two (i.e., G Major to F Major.)

EX. 14.1c – "Yankee Doodle," scored for piano or other concert-pitched instrument, notated in tenor clef.

Now practice your transposition with three excerpts by Weber. Be careful of accidentals in **Ex. 14.2**: the first two notes of the following excerpt sound as E♭ and B♭, not E and B! For this reason it is important to identify the transposed key. **Ex. 14.2** is written in the key of F Major, but will sound a whole step lower in the key of E♭ Major.

EX. 14.2 – Weber, Concertino for Clarinet and Orchestra, Op. 26, mm. 38–42. B♭ clarinet part excerpted.

When you first begin reading transposing instruments, it may be helpful to write in a couple of notes to keep your transposition on track. In **Ex. 14.3**, for example, it might be helpful to write in "E" above the downbeat of the second measure, and "A♭" above the second beat of the fourth measure. Both of these notes occur after jumps, which can cause problems for those new to transposition! If you do resort to writing in some note names be sure to limit it to one or two per example. If you write in all the note names you will only be reading the note names and will not be practicing your skills at transposition.

EX. 14.3 – Weber, Concerto in F minor for Clarinet and Orchestra, Op. 73, movt. II, mm. 1–5. B♭ clarinet part excerpted.

As in earlier chapters, it can be helpful to identify significant intervals. In **Ex. 14.4**, quickly mark in any leaps of octaves and fifths you see.

EX. 14.4 – Weber, Concerto in F minor for Clarinet and Orchestra, Op. 73, movt. III, mm. 174–184. B♭ clarinet part excerpted.

Now that you are comfortable playing these parts, try putting them together with concert-pitched, accompanimental parts.

EX. 14.5 – Weber, Concertino for Clarinet and Orchestra, Op. 26, mm. 38–42. B♭ clarinet and cello parts excerpted.

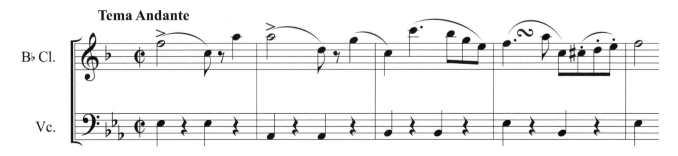

EX. 14.6 – Weber, Concerto in F minor for Clarinet and Orchestra, Op. 73, movt. II, mm. 1–5. B♭ clarinet and cello parts excerpted.

EX. 14.7 – Weber, Concerto in F minor for Clarinet and Orchestra, Op. 73, movt. 3, mm. 174–184. B♭ clarinet and violin II parts excerpted.

Note: In this excerpt you may perform the tremolos in the violin II part as a series of eighth notes.

2 Sight-reading Exercises

For each sight-reading exercise, quickly look over the excerpt first, making note of possible trouble spots. If you have significant trouble reading the transposing instrumental part, try writing in a couple of notes.

EX. 14.8 – Beethoven, Trio in B♭ Major for Piano, Clarinet, and Cello, Op. 11, movt. III, Var. IV, mm. 1–15. Clarinet and cello parts excerpted.

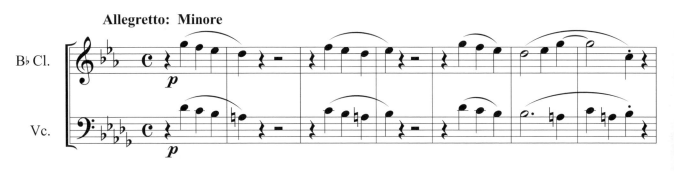

In this excerpt note where the parts move in parallel thirds or in unisons.

EX. 14.9 – Mozart, *Serenade*, No. 12, KV 388, movt. 4, mm. 100–111. Clarinet and bassoon parts excerpted.

EX. 14.10 – Bach, "Domine Deus," from Mass in G Major, arr. by Moritz, mm. 1–11.

EX. 14.11 – Haydn, Octet in F Major, movt. II, mm. 1–16. Clarinet and cello parts excerpted.

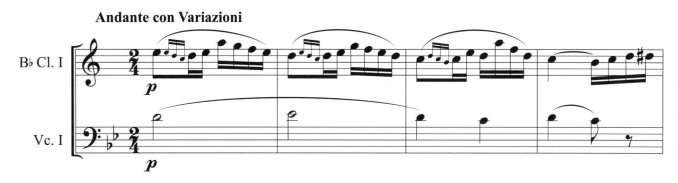

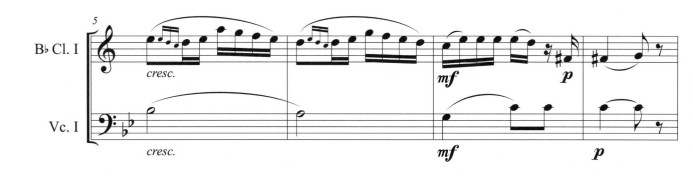

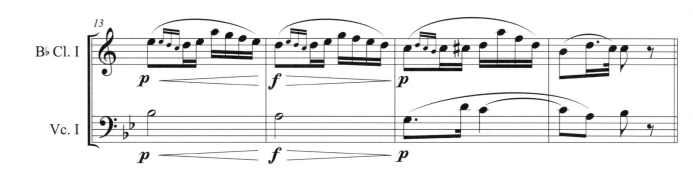

3 Prepared Exercises

For each prepared exercise, the full score has been given and you are asked to perform two or more parts from the score. Feel free to make markings in the score to facilitate your performance.

EX. 14.12 – Beethoven, Trio in B♭ Major for Piano, Clarinet, and Cello, Op. 11, movt. III, Var. II, mm. 1–17.

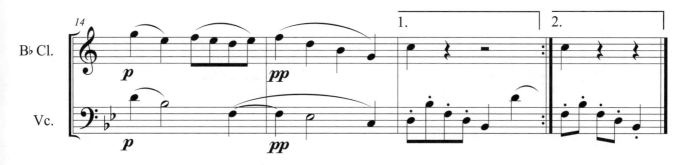

Make note of the imitation between the clarinet and cello parts and use this feature to assist in the transposition of the clarinet part.

EX. 14.13 – Haydn, Octet in F Major, movt. III, mm. 1–18. Oboe I, B♭ clarinet I, and bassoon II parts excerpted.

In this excerpt perform the clarinet part with either the oboe or bassoon parts.

EX. 14.14 – Schubert, Octet in F Major, Op. 166, movt. II, mm. 1–11. B♭ clarinet, violin II, and cello parts excerpted.

EX. 14.15 – Mozart, *Serenade No. 12*, KV 388, movt. I, mm. 48–60. Oboe, clarinet, and bassoon parts excerpted.

Note: In this excerpt the final oboe note has been revised to provide a concluding perfect authentic cadence.

Perform trumpet and cello parts, then trumpet, cello and violin II.

EX. 14.16 – Berlioz, *Symphonie Fantastique*, movt. V, mm. 414–434. Strings and B♭ trumpet excerpted.

EX. 14.16 – continued

EX. 14.16 – continued

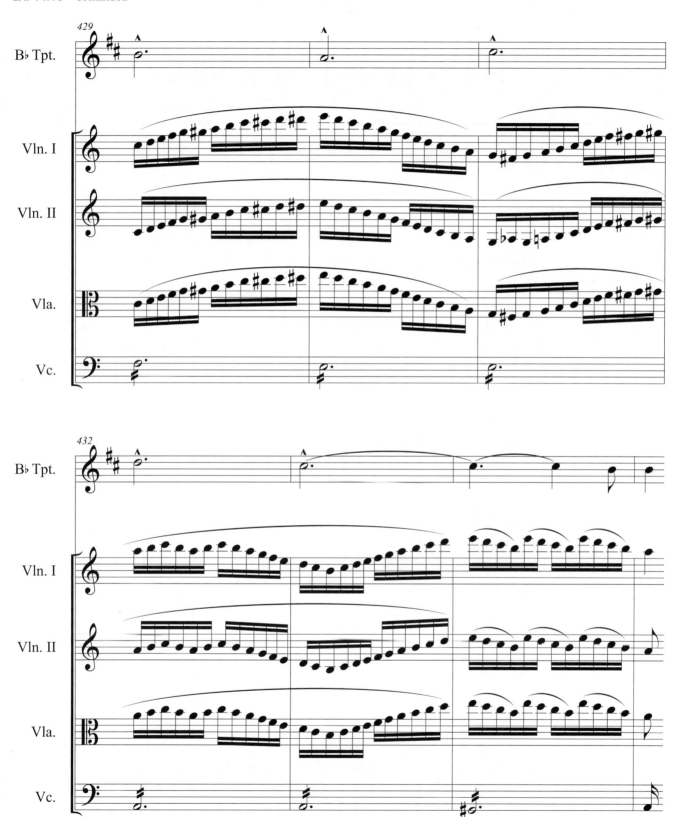

Chapter 15

E♭ Transposing Instruments

1 Introduction

After B♭ transpositions, the most common transposition you will encounter is E♭. Alto and baritone saxophones, some horns, and some clarinets are E♭ transposing instruments, so it will be helpful if you are comfortable reading this transposition. The general rule for any E♭ transposing instrument is that when reading a C in the score, the sounding pitch will be an E♭. In some cases, you will be transposing up a minor third, and at other times you will be transposing down a major sixth.

- E♭ instruments sounding a minor third *higher*

  - Soprano Clarinet
  - E♭ Trumpet
  - Sopranino Saxophone

- E♭ instruments sounding a major sixth *lower*

  - Alto Saxophone
  - Alto Clarinet
  - E♭ Horn

- E♭ instrument sounding a major sixth plus one octave *lower*

  - Baritone Saxophone

In **Ex. 15.1a,** a short melody is provided. If this part were written for an E♭ transposing instrument, it would sound in the key of E♭ major, but the octave in which the melody sounds would differ depending on which E♭ instrument performed the melody.

EX. 15.1a – Traditional, "For He's a Jolly Good Fellow."

First try transposing "For He's a Jolly Good Fellow" to sound at concert pitch when performed by an Eb trumpet. In this situation you will need to transpose the melody up a minor third. To check your accuracy, look at **Ex. 15.b,** which is written at concert pitch for this instrument.

EX. 15.1b – Traditional, "For He's a Jolly Good Fellow," concert pitch for Eb trumpet.

Now try transposing **Ex. 15.1a,** "For He's a Jolly Good Fellow," to sound at concert pitch when performed by an alto saxophone. You will still transpose the melody to the key of Eb major, but the melody will sound a major sixth lower. To check your accuracy, look at **Ex. 15.1c.**

EX. 15.1c – Traditional, "For He's a Jolly Good Fellow," concert pitch for alto saxophone.

Finally, imagine that **Ex. 15.1a,** "For He's a Jolly Good Fellow," was scored for a baritone saxophone and perform the melody at concert pitch. In this case you will transpose the original melody down a major sixth plus an additional octave. You transposition should sound like **Ex. 15.1d.**

EX. 15.1d – Traditional, "For He's a Jolly Good Fellow," concert pitch for baritone saxophone.

Now, compare the original notation of "For He's a Jolly Good Fellow" in **Ex. 15.1a** with **Ex. 15.1d**. Although the clefs are different, you should notice that the pitches for each example line up on the same lines and spaces in the staff. This feature can assist you with any E♭ transposition. When transposing an E♭ instrument part notated in treble clef, you may read the original notation, but "think" in bass clef and apply the appropriate accidentals for the concert pitch key. This new key signature will involve adding three flats to the original key signature, removing three sharps, or a combination of the two. The last step is to ensure that the melody is performed in the proper octave.

2 Sight-reading Exercises

For each of the following excerpts, briefly look over the score before playing, identifying key areas, problem spots, parallel intervals, unisons, etc. Once you begin playing, try not to stop or hesitate. Refer back to the list of E♭ transposing instruments if you are not sure whether to transpose up a third or down a sixth.

EX. 15.2 – Mozart, Horn Concerto in E♭, movt. I, mm. 91–98. Solo horn and cello parts excerpted.

Note: the key signature has been adjusted to match the key of the excerpt.

EX. 15.3 – Haydn, Trumpet Concerto in E♭, movt. I, mm. 105–109. Solo trumpet and cello parts excerpted.

Sight-read the saxophone and left hand of the piano. Also try reading the saxophone an octave higher with the right hand of the piano for an added challenge!

EX. 15.4 – Traditional, "Auld Lang Syne," arr. Moritz, mm. 1–8.

Sight-read bassoon and E♭ horn parts only. For an added challenge combine the horn and clarinet parts.

EX. 15.5 – Mozart, *Serenade*, K. 388, movt. I, mm. 48–60. E♭ horn, B♭ clarinet, and bassoon parts excerpted.

3 Prepared Exercises

For each of the following, prepare all parts, or the specified selection of parts from the score. Feel free to write in indications to help your performance.

Prepare the horn part with either the left hand or right hand of the piano.

EX. 15.6 – Danzi, Sonata in E♭, movt. II, mm. 21–29.

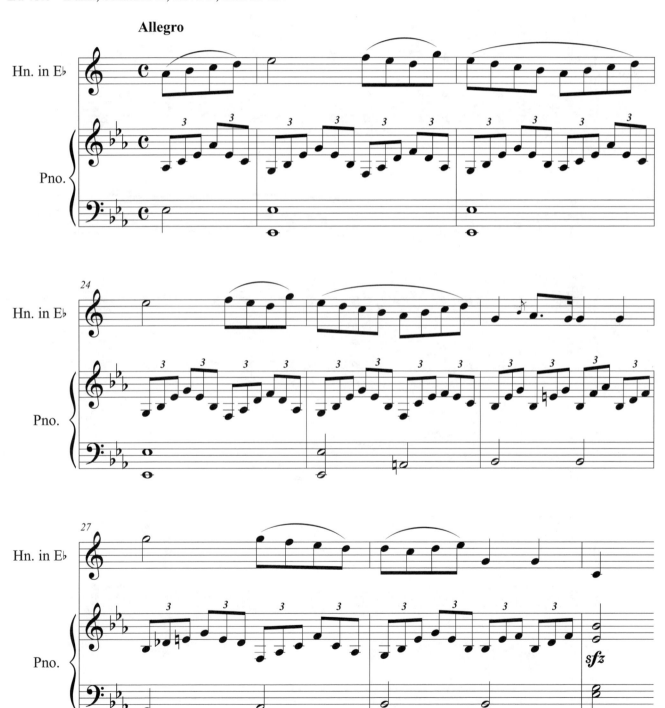

Prepare trumpet and piano LH parts only.

EX. 15.7 – Haydn, Trumpet Concerto in E♭, movt. II, mm. 1–18.

EX. 15.7 – continued

For the following exercise, the same excerpt is provided, but in full score rather than a piano reduction. Use your familiarity with **Ex. 15.7** to help you with **Ex. 15.8**.

Prepare trumpet and violins I and II.

EX. 15.8 – Haydn, Trumpet Concerto in E♭, movt. II, mm. 1–18, full score.

EX. 15.8 – continued

Begin with learning to play the horn part with the cello/bass parts. Then try performing the horn part with the upper strings, omitting the cello/bass parts. In this situation you will need to transpose the horn up an octave to avoid overlap with the strings.

EX. 15.9 – Mozart, Horn Concerto in E♭, K. 447, movt. II, mm. 1–8.

EX. 15.10 – Arma, "Divertimento No. 18," mm. 1–17.

Prepare horn; with your left hand play as many of the string parts as you can.

EX. 15.11 – Haydn, Symphony in E♭, No. 22, movt. III, mm. 33–52. Horn and string parts excerpted.

EX. 15.11 – continued

The soprano and tenor saxophones are both B♭ instruments, but the tenor saxophone needs to be transposed down an additional octave. The same relationship holds true for the alto and baritone saxophones. Both are E♭ instruments, which transpose down a major sixth, but the baritone saxophone needs to be transposed down an additional octave.

EX. 15.12 – Young, *Saxophone Quartet*, movt. III, mm. 1–16.

EX. 15.12 – continued

EX. 15.13 – McMichael, "Sarabande," from *Eclectic Trio*, mm. 1–17.

Chapter 16

F and A Transposing Instruments

1 Introduction

In this final chapter you will have the opportunity to practice reading F and A transposing instruments. The most common F instrument is the French horn, although English horns and basset horns are also frequently in F. These instruments sound a perfect fifth lower than the notated pitch. Instruments that sound a minor third lower than concert pitch (A instruments) include the A clarinet, A trumpet, and the oboe d'amore. Of these the A clarinet is the most common.

In addition to a gradual introduction to these transpositions, this chapter also includes opportunities to read several different transposing instruments at the same time.

Many people find that transpositions down a perfect fifth or a minor third are among the most difficult given that there is no easily available clef substitution trick such as those discussed in Chapters 14 and 15. If you are skilled in *solfege* or scale degree numbers you can use this ability to assist with transposition. The next four examples illustrate the opening measures of "Twinkle, Twinkle, Little Star." Try thinking of the solfege syllables for the given melody, then apply these syllables to the concert pitch key to determine the needed pitches. The following exercise will test your F transposition—to check your accuracy, the following two exercises (**Ex. 16.1a and b**) should sound identical.

EX. 16.1a – "Twinkle, Twinkle, Little Star," mm. 1–4, scored for horn in F.

EX. 16.1b – "Twinkle, Twinkle, Little Star," mm. 1–4, for concert-pitched instrument.

Now try your A transpositions. Remember, A instruments always transpose *down* a minor third. As with the pervious example, think of the solfege syllables in the given key of C major and transfer these syllables into letter names in the concert pitch key of A major.

EX. 16.2a – "Twinkle, Twinkle, Little Star," mm. 1–4, scored for oboe d'amore.

Oboe
d'Amore

EX. 16.2b – "Twinkle, Twinkle, Little Star," mm. 1–4, for concert-pitched instrument.

Concert
Pitch

2 Sight-reading Exercises

In the following exercises, be sure to identify the interval of transposition first. You may write in a note name at the beginning, or after a leap, as you begin reading these transpositions. As you progress, try to write in less and less.

EX. 16.3 – Nielsen, Quintet, Op. 43, movt. IV, Var. IX, mm. 1–8. The horn is solo in this variation.

Note: This melody primarily features an arpeggiation through a C major triad. Although there is one sharp in the key signature, the notated pitches easily conform to the key of C major. When transposed down a perfect fifth, this triad will sound as an F major triad.

Before transposing the clarinet part, try singing the melody on solfege or scale degree numbers. When you are ready to begin transposing, sing the melody with solfege or scale degree numbers while playing the melody transposed to the key of A major.

EX 16.4 – Mozart, Clarinet Concerto, KV 622, movt. III, mm. 36–39, clarinet and violin II parts excerpted.

First sight-read the horn and bassoon parts, then try reading the clarinet and horn parts.

EX. 16.5 – Haydn, Octet, movt. III, mm. 5–8.

Note: In this example the score order has been revised, moving the bassoon part below the horn part to avoid the appearance of voice crossing at this point in the chapter.

EX. 16.6 – Schubert, Octet, Op. 166, movt. V, mm. 47–51.

In this excerpt the final note of the violin II part has been altered to provide an effective ending to the example.

EX. 16.7 – Mozart, Clarinet Concerto, K 622, movt. III, mm. 116–121, clarinet and violin II parts excerpted.

EX. 16.8 – Haydn, Octet, movt. II, Var. 3, mm. 1–8, horn and cello excerpted.

EX. 16.9 – Nielsen, Quintet, movt. III, theme. A clarinet and bassoon parts excerpted.

3 Prepared Exercises

For each of the following excerpts, be sure to write in markings to help with your performance. As in previous transposition chapters, avoid writing in too many note names. One or two note names after large leaps or at the beginning of an excerpt can be helpful, but excessive indications will slow the development of your transposition skills.

EX. 16.10 – Schubert, Octet, Op. 166, movt. I, mm. 61–71.

EX. 16.10 – continued

Note that both instruments transpose!

EX. 16.11 – Ewald, Quintet, No. 2, movt. II, var. I, mm. 9–16. Trumpet II and horn parts excerpted.

EX. 16.12 – Haydn, Octet, movt. III, mm. 19–34, clarinet I, horn I and bassoon II parts excerpted.

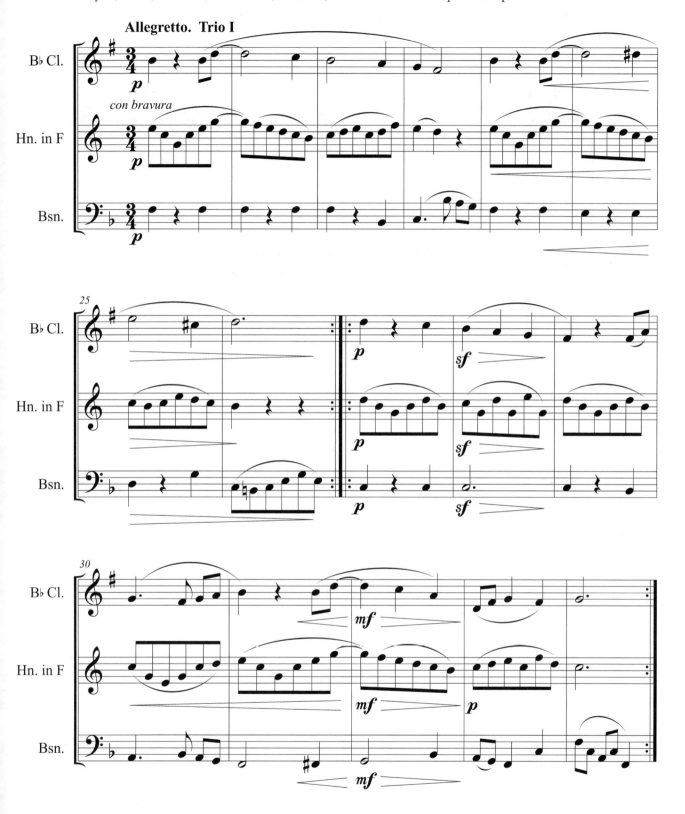

After learning the horn part, pair it up with either the B♭ clarinet or the bassoon part. Be sure to note the places where the clarinet and horn are in unison and where the parts cross.

Prepare all parts. Note that the horn is first paired with two concert-pitched instruments, then with two B♭ instruments.

EX. 16.13 – Scheidt, arr. De Jong, *Canzona Bergamasca*, mm. 68–73.

EX. 16.13 – continued

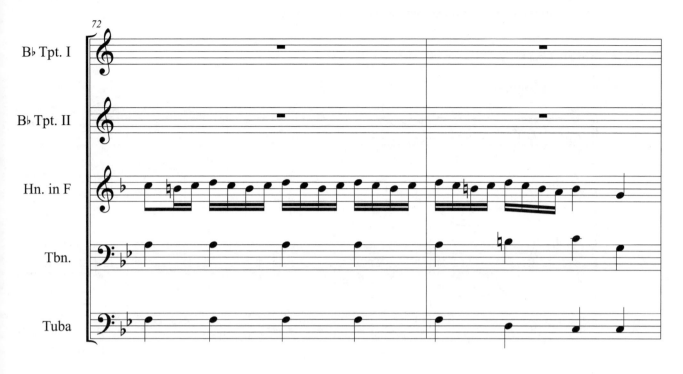

First prepare the clarinet and cello parts. Then try pairing the clarinet with each of the other string parts. Be careful: the violin I and clarinet parts frequently create unisons.

EX. 16.14 – Mozart, Quintet, K 581, movt. II, mm. 51–70.

EX. 16.14 – continued

Prepare various parts in combination with one another.

EX. 16.15 – Nielsen, Quintet, Op. 43, movt. III, theme, mm. 1–16.

Tema con variazioni: Un poco andantino

EX. 16.15 – continued

Note: For the theme of this set of variations Nielsen substituted the English Horn in place of the oboe. Do you remember the english horn transposition? (See the beginning of the chapter.)

Prepare all parts.

EX. 16.16 – Ewazen, *Colchester Fantasy*, movt. II, "The Marquis of Granby," mm. 1–23.

EX. 16.16 – continued

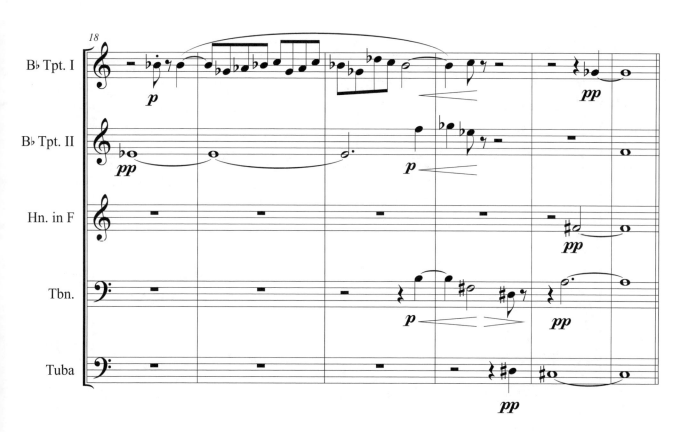

Prepare various parts in combination with one another.

EX. 16.17 – Nielsen, Quintet, movt. III, Var. VI, mm. 1–16.

EX. 16.17 – continued

Play all parts.

EX. 16.18 – Ewald, Quintet, No. 2, movt. III, mm. 1–9.

Appendix

Choral Warm-Up Exercises

Involving the piano in your choral warm-ups can be very beneficial. In addition to providing the pitch, a well-played accompaniment can create energy in your choir and better engage your singers in the process. Several standard choral warm-ups are listed below, along with suggested keyboard accompaniments. Lyrics and syllables have been omitted in these warm-ups—the choir director should use his/her discretion to choose appropriate syllables for these exercises.

Each warm-up pattern concludes with the dominant seventh chord in the key a half step higher to assist in moving up the chromatic scale. When descending chromatically you will need to modify each segment by concluding with the dominant seventh chord in the key a half step below.

Note: The basic chord progressions described in these warm-ups can be used to support numerous other warm-ups as well, so even if you would prefer to do different warm-ups, it will still be worth your time to prepare the following accompaniments.

The first three keys are given; continue transposing up a half step as far as needed.

WARM-UP 1 – Descending thirds with I–V accompaniment.

WARM-UP 1 – continued

continue pattern

WARM-UP 2 – Up and Down Scale with I–IV–I–V accompaniment.

WARM-UP 2 – continued

WARM-UP 3 – Ascending arpeggio and descending scale.

WARM-UP 3 – continued

Note: One possible realization of the chords is given here. Feel free to experiment with different patterns and inversions.

WARM-UP 4 – Leap of a fifth and ascending scale.

WARM-UP 4 – continued

Two different accompanimental patterns have been provided. These can be mixed and matched with other warm-ups as well.

WARM-UP 5 – Ascending and descending arpeggio.

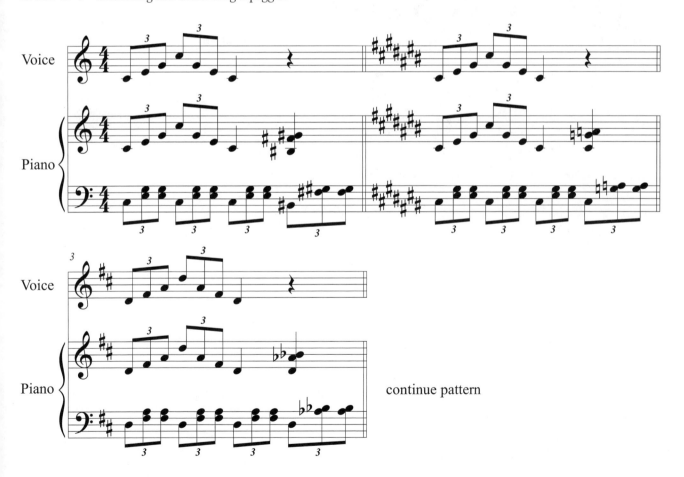

continue pattern

WARM-UP 5 – continued

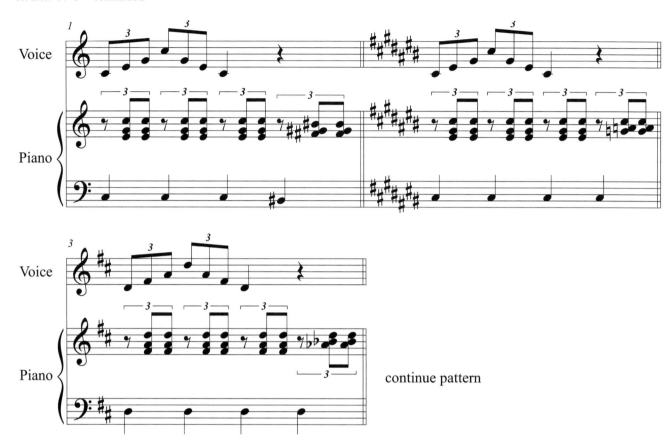

continue pattern

Index of Excerpts